WHY NO WEIGHT LOSS?

Weight, imbalance and food intolerance

LIZ TUCKER

Contents

WHY WEIGHT?

For decades dieting has dominated the nations eating habits but in spite of this we now have the highest rates of obesity ever in this country. This result is even more surprising when you consider the fact that we all seem to know the very simple solution of eating less and exercising more. It seems the more people harp on about the relationship between calories and fuel expenditure the less it seems to work. If we assume that nobody likes carrying excessive amounts of fat and all the negative aspects it carries with it then why are so many people struggling with this simple equation?

There is no doubt that an element of today's weight problems are simply to do with too much extremely edible food with very little effort to get it but are we really that stupid and lazy?

IS THIS YOU?

Questionnaire

Tip

Have a pencil and paper handy so you can take part in exercises throughout the book.

- Are you unhappy with your weight?

- Have you felt like this for more than a year?

- Have you tried to diet at least 5 times without success?

- How does it effect your life?

- Why does it upset you?

- Do you blame other problems in your life on your weight?

- Are you a fad diet fanatic?

- Does dieting dominate your life?

ARE WE LAZY?

Not if you consider that the other major complaint of modern living is it is just too busy. For many the demands of family, home and work are becoming increasingly harder to balance. Apparently we are a nation who is on the go all the time, burdened by stress and endless fatigue and because this is not good for our health we are also having to find even more time to retain some level of fitness. Taking care of our health is becoming detached from everyday living.

Describe your day
Is it:

A
- Early start as so much to do
- Take kids to school
- Rush into work
- Shopping lunch time
- Pick up kids
- Frantic clean round the house
- Eat late
- Never have an early night

B
- Find it hard to get up
- Find it hard to get motivated
- Find work boring
- Comfort eat
- Don't socialize
- Feel tired even though you haven't done anything
- Fall asleep in front of the TV

If it's

A - busy
Then your body will be finding it hard to keep up with your energy demands and food could be just a quick fix energy prop.

B - not busy
Then your physical and emotional state are not coping with the demands of everyday living and food could be your main source of relief.

Either way it's not just about calories!

ARE WE STUPID?

Today's society is generally better educated, we have greater access to health advice and information about our food and we can't all be ignoring it. Also the majority are not obese, most people who class themselves as being overweight, dislike their shape or find maintaining a healthy weight a problem. You may probably only want to lose half a stone or that completely out of proportion piece of fat on the side of your thighs and have tried unsuccessfully for years to shift it permanently.

If you have been trying to lose weight, look better and feel fitter and healthier but failing miserably, the onus being on the word miserable, then you will have already worked out that there is something more to it than the simple equation of calories and exercise. So if it is not just that, what else is there?

Well basically there is you!

Basics of good health advice

- Eat 5 bits of fruit and veg a day
- Drink 2 litres of water
- Exercise 30 mins - 5 times week
- Reduce your fat, salt, refined carbohydrates and sugar intake

Over a week – chart how many times you actually achieve these targets

- Be honest with your answers.
- If you follow less than 2 then your overall diet needs rebalancing.
- If you follow more than 2 then there may be other lifestyle factors involved such as stress.
- If you think you follow all 5 then there could be a biological imbalance and you need to find a diet that suits your individuality.

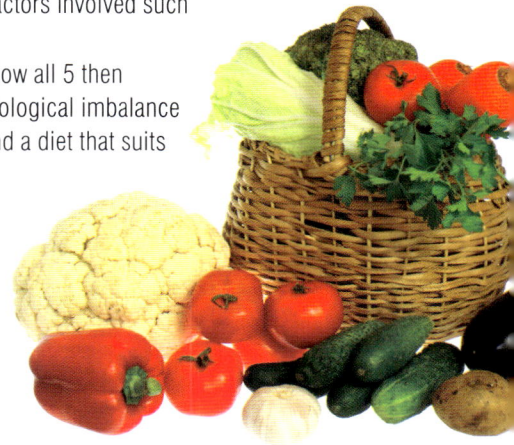

YOU ARE UNIQUE

When we look at health we need to consider two aspects. The first one is that human bodies are fundamentally all the same. We have the same cellular structure, circulatory system and need of nutrients and this is where general health advice applies. We can say to stay slim we all need to eat less and exercise more because biologically this is how it works but the emphasis here is on the word generally because the second aspect is your uniqueness. Your biological identity could mean that general rules don't always apply so effectively. The body is extremely complex and so is the process of putting it together. Variations in makeup occur because although the basic standard components need to be there to make a human body, the circumstances of your creation are unique. This means that aspects of your manufacture and functioning are unique to you. Some bits of you work better, worse or differently to other peoples. For example generally all hormonal levels, blood pressure, metabolism, nutritional absorption and bone density fit into a standard range but each individual reading is going to be slightly different or even out of the range. We also have variations in our thought processes and responses depending firstly on our genetic mix and secondly, differences in our environment and upbringing. With so many complex systems in the body and environmental factors to consider, the odds of two people having everything exactly the same is almost incalculable. Each life is individual, you are unique.

What makes you, you?

List your

Likes:	Thin waist	Good organizer	Loyal friend
Dislikes:	Impatient	Lack stamina	Big hips

The same or not?

Quiz

[1]

A

Do you always agree and let everyone have their own way?

B

Get angry if you can't do your own thing and find it hard to work in a team?

[2]

A

Like your own company and are intolerant of other people?

B

Do you like being one of the crowd and lead a very social life?

[3]

A

Do you tend to like the same food as your friends and family?

B

Are there certain foods you avoid even though everyone else seems to love them?

Actually there are no right or wrong answers. There may be certain answers that are more relevant to you but actually most of you would say that both answers apply depending on how you feel. So there is something the same in all of us but ultimately you are unique.

FOOD FOR LIFE

Food is essential. Even at a basic level we all know that we need food to stay alive but our nutritional requirements for health and fitness are much more complex. Most people know that food is essential for fuel but we often forget that we are actually made from the nutritional components we get from food. Every bit of your body from its manufacture to maintenance is totally reliant on nutrients. All our cellular structures including bones, muscles and organs, our blood and brain, are made from nutrients such as the protein and fat we get from food. All our bodily functions will only occur because we give them the right mix of vitamins and minerals. It seems too obvious to say this but we need a healthy, varied, balanced diet, to make a healthy body. There is no way round it, if you don't provide your body with the right mix of nutritional components then it will struggle to function and maintain itself. As with everything in the body, nutrients need to interrelate to function effectively. Individual nutrients in isolation do not work, there needs to be balance. Too much of the same food will give you an overload in some nutrients, creating waste, storage and disposal problems for the body and a deficiency in others making the stack of ones you have got of little value.

Two main reasons why we need food

- **Energy** - food provides us with the energy we need to live. Energy is not just about enabling you to move or think, most of our energy is used in bodily functions such as digestion and immune responses. We are made from trillions of cells and each one needs energy to power it.

- **Body building** - food provides us with the essential components we need to make our body in the first place, keep it in good repair and enable it to function.

FAT FOOD

When it comes to weight the first thing we think of is calories and that calories are bad. Calories are not bad, they are simply a way of measuring the amount of potential energy in individual foods. Simply put, 1 calorie equals 1 unit of energy so rather than being a bad thing a calorie is your energy supply. The problem is if we don't use that energy it gets stored as fat. Basically fat cells are empty storage containers that fill up with potential energy in the form of fat. When we need further energy and there is no food available, we utilize this fat so fat cells swell up and empty out depending on our energy output requirements, changing our size and shape in the process. It is during our childhood development that we manufacture fat cells. Unfortunately if you were over weight as a child you will have developed above average numbers of fat cells so it will be harder for you to stay slim in adulthood but not impossible. If you were an average slim child then your weight gain at maturity is more to do with existing fat cells getting bigger rather than the production of new ones.

What overweight range are you in?

Small
Less than a stone or 6 kilos and a key area of fat imbalance such as hips or waist

Medium
1 to 2 stone overweight or 6 to 12 kilos

Large
Over 3 stone overweight or 12 kilos

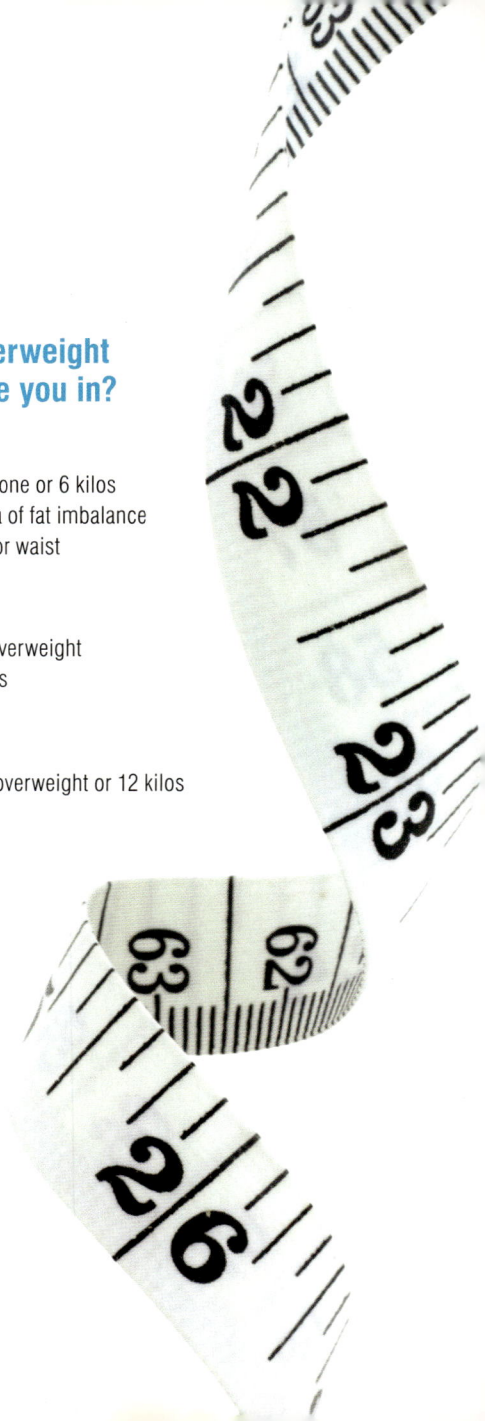

We also have to consider that not all calories are the same. As carbohydrate and fat are our main source of energy these are the nutrients we are more likely to store as fat. Proteins and certain fats are used to build and maintain body parts so they are more likely to be utilised than stored as fat. Different carbohydrates can be fast or slow burning depending on the chemical makeup. Sugars burn immediately as they are so close to pure glucose which gives an immediate energy boost. Unfortunately high intakes can also produce biological imbalances such as excessive insulin production leading to glucose intolerance, diabetes, adrenal and thyroid problems which can all negatively influence not just your health but also your shape and weight. Slow release unrefined carbohydrates such as wholemeal cereals give us more consistent energy and retain healthy blood sugar levels but are harder to process and high intakes can overload the digestive system, potentially encouraging fluid retention, bloating, constipation and leaving it prone to IBS, food intolerance and bacterial problems.

Not all calories are the same

- The more muscle you have the more calories you will burn even if you are not moving
- Half a kilo of muscle burns 50 more calories a day than fat tissue
- 1g fat contains 9 calories but 1g carbohydrate or protein has only 4

Theoretically the more calories you consume the more energy you should have available to use but we all know there is something wrong with this equation. With so many of us the more we eat the fatter we become and the less energy this seems to produce. In this case weight problems can be seen as a symptom of some sort of ongoing internal imbalance which unless rectified will continue no matter how much you try to gain and retain healthy weight and shape. In fact low calorie, yo-yo and fad diets could be increasing or sustaining this imbalance leading to a terrible spiral of frustration and misery when nothing seems to work. In order to examine this further we need to look away from the basic biology and more into the complex nature of your individual make up.

To lose weight firstly you must accept that intake and output is still a big part of the jigsaw but without locating the other missing pieces you could struggle to find the weight and energy you so desperately crave. Trying to lose weight, get fitter and healthier can be a very frustrating and demoralising experience especially when you think you are doing all the right things to make it happen. You would think your body would be pleased with your efforts to get healthy so why does it throw in sabotaging nasties like food craving, bloating, fluid retention and fatigue?

This book aims to address simply some of the more complex theories relating to your weight and health such as food intolerance, energy imbalances and poor digestive processing that are more relevant to you as an individual. If you are fed up with diets that don't work now is the time to find the food that works for you.

Remember...

when it comes to
your weight and shape

- You are unique
- Not just about calories

PERFECTLY IMPERFECT

When it comes to weight the first thing you need to ask yourself is do you really need to lose weight?

I have asked many people with weight and body shape issues over the years what is the one thing they would most like to change and the vast majority say they would like more energy. Weight is a secondary issue, what most of you are really fed up with is feeling tired and run down and excess fat is getting the blame for it. Of course being overweight is an obvious reason why you might feel exhausted but only if you know you are unfit and seriously overweight. Ironically if you could magic more energy out of the air, increases in metabolism would probably provide you with the sustainable healthy shape and weight you want and then there wouldn't be a problem. So if you want to lose weight or improve your shape, improving your health is the most important factor and not counting calories.

Apart from more energy being on top of most peoples wish list, being in control comes a close second. With many it is not about their actual weight at this point in time but the inability to control it and keep it stable over the years. You may only be putting on a few pounds a year or constantly fluctuating by half a stone but the inability to control something as simple as your weight generates real panic about your ability to do anything successfully, knocking confidence and creating fear for your future stability.

Many of you only want to lose 5 kilos or reduce the size of your hips and having no energy is not going to help you shift this. Also if you lack energy any additional weight or imperfections in shape are going to feel in your tired mind so much bigger because your self-esteem is taking a bashing. Basically for an accurate account of how much weight you need to lose and what body shape you should have, you are probably the last person to ask. For example, today's trend for being super skinny is neither healthy or attractive but women in particular aspire to it and are prepared to put their health at risk to achieve this unnatural state. Being too thin is equally bad for your body and leaves you feeling awful so what weight is the right weight for you and your health?

What's your Weight Distribution
Your shape can be a clue to where the problem lies

- **Apple** – insulin resistance, bacterial or food intolerance could add weight in this area
- **Pear** – Fluid retention, toxins and stress can add weight here
- **All over** – poor energy production and metabolic problems can lead to problems here

The simple answer is the size and shape you should be aiming to achieve is the one that leaves you feeling good. Rather than viewing your size and weight as "the" problem see them more as a resulting symptom of a negative factor in your lifestyle, internal biology, environment, mental state or more usually a combination. It is unlikely there is just one thing but more a catalogue of small but negative imbalances over time that conspire against you, generating one big persistent problem. Find your combination of imbalances and you will feel more in control, know how to boost energy and ultimately gain and retain the size and shape that is right for your own personal health and well-being.

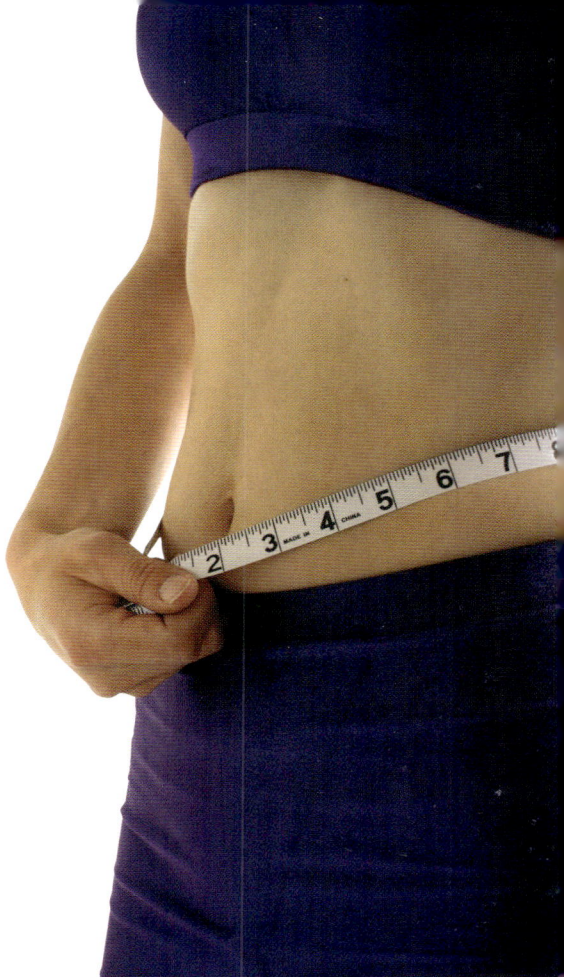

Types of Imbalances

- Lifestyle
- Stress
- Diet
- Alcohol
- Smoking
- Mental state

- Low confidence
- Self esteem
- Unhappy
- Environment
- Pollution
- Financial worry

- Poor relationship
- Biological
- Blood glucose
- Food intolerance
- Low metabolism

WORKING WITH YOUR BODY

Do you work with your natural balance?

- When you are busy do you forget to drink?
- When you feel unhappy do you ignore it?
- When you feel tired do you just try and carry on?
- Do you think your lifestyle makes it hard for you to keep fit?
- Where does your health fit on your list of daily priorities?
- Do you only think about your body when its not working well?
- Do you feel guilty about taking time out to relax or have fun?

Your body knows what it needs to do to stay healthy but it can't do it without your help. This is the deal. Its role is to keep all your internal systems up and running, supply you with energy, cope with constant change, keep you safe, offer the best advice, put up with your environment and deal with your constant demands. Your role is simply to supply it with the right resources and circumstances to enable it to do just that. With so many things to consider its not surprising that imbalances occur. Unfortunately the negative effects of one imbalance if prolonged can start to generate further problems until you find yourself unable to control a spiral of growing negativity. For example your job is under threat, you worry more, you comfort eat, you put weight on, you feel tired, you feel hungry all the time so you eat more, then you feel unhappy about

how you look, stop going out so you stay in and comfort eat. Your external reactions to the initial problem if prolonged can then undermine your internal health. For example stress, poor diet and lack of positive stimulation can start to overload the adrenal glands, weaken gut actions and over sensitise the nervous system while lack of good nutrition and little sleep will starve the body of the resources it so desperately needs to cope with the problems generated. What started out as an isolated problem with work soon undermines your entire health and well-being. At this point it is almost as if your body is trying to conspire against your efforts to improve your health. But under pressure it will have no choice but to take emergency measures that may well deal with the immediate problem but ultimately be damaging long term.

Are you listening?

- You have the usual 3.30pm energy slump - do you grab chocolate and coffee or drink water and have a break?
- After a busy day - do you have a glass of wine and fall asleep in front of the TV or soak in the bath and go to bed early?
- If something upsets you - do you raid the fridge or go for a walk with a friend?

Why No Weight Loss?

BALANCE

The body functions through a system of balance called Homeostasis. Daily, hourly, even every second throughout life our body has to deal with constant change. In order to survive the body has developed an elaborate feedback system to enable it to keep on an even keel. For example, if it is short of fluid it will retain it, too much and it will flush it out, so you will be either instructed by your brain to drink more or go to the toilet. But not all bodies are equal so our ability to successfully balance things varies. For example some will be better at temperature control while others struggle to keep warm. Your biological strengths and weaknesses are not set in genetic stone, you and your environment can seriously influence your body's ability to keep things in balance. A scary situation might suddenly appear out of the blue or you might decide to work late when your body has had enough but it will still rise to the occasion knowing it will de-stabilise your internal system. It relies on the fact that it can put things right later when the problem is over. So just because you are born with a weakness or difference does not mean to say it will be a problem it only means it could become a problem if other negative things happen in your life.

There are thousands of functions and circumstances the body needs to keep in check and on the whole, even with it's own little built in weaknesses it does a fantastic job. One of the greatest imbalancing influences is the state of your health, the healthier you are, the less likely it is for your body to become imbalanced. Therefore the more you understand and accept your own individuality, the easier it is to keep the balance. In many cases we know what we are doing to upset the system, such as smoking or drinking too much, but find it hard to accept we need to change, hoping we will be the unlikely one who will get away with it. What is really frustrating is when you think you are looking after yourself and it seems to make no difference but there are still some internal, biological imbalances that can still occur and I hope to address some of these in this book.

Lifestyle imbalances

- Smoking
- Bad diet
- Stress overload
- Low activity levels

Internal imbalances

- Food intolerance
- Gut bacteria ratio .
- Insulin intolerance
- Unfortunately both imbalances can influence each other

HERE'S THE PLAN

Firstly this book focuses on ways the body works, what goes on inside, what's the same, what's different and how that can lead to weight problems. The next section looks more at how you influence the way your body works and the final part offers a plan of action and suggestions about what you can do to help yourself. Basically the body is a system of moving and functioning parts that need constant maintenance and resources but none of us start off on a level playing field. We all have in-built weaknesses that make some things harder to manage such as maintaining a healthy weight. We all know calories play a part in the size and shape we are but there must be more to it than just fat. For example fluid retention, inflammation and bloating all add weight and inches. Part one looks at some of the theories behind these unpleasant symptoms. Some are well-documented biology others are based on new but still developing lines of research. But I don't want to get bogged down in science, while avoiding the real wacky my aim is to suggest a range of theories and let you chose if any relate to you.

Your first clues

- You have followed endless weight loss diets and still have a weight problem
- Have other health or energy problems
- Notice any change for better or worse when you changed your diet
- Have any negative reactions after eating, such as bloating
- Find it hard to stay motivated
- Find that life just gets in the way of staying healthy

WHEN THINGS DON'T WORK

Three things to remember

1 – Things don't happen in isolation. There is a complex biological balancing system going on in the body which means there is likely to be more than one thing to consider. You will need to unpick and address each imbalance that relates to you in order to solve the overall problem. Some can be sorted but some things may always be a weakness but once recognised can be better managed. Some may never be found but dealing with the majority will dilute their impact.

2 – Your body needs you. For decades diet has just meant calorie reduction and this has created a very unhealthy and unsustainable mindset regarding what is and isn't right to eat. The dramatic rise in mass-produced convenience foods, low in nutritional value have distanced us further from our natural instinct to eat the right diet. Also modern medicine has become so successful at suppressing negative symptoms that many of us have stopped listening to our body. Combine all this with today's busy lifestyles and we are not giving ourselves time to assess if our body is happy and address what is wrong. Negative symptoms such as pain and weight gain are our body's way of telling us something is out of balance. All the clues are there if we stopped to listen.

3 – Look inside. If you have been struggling for years to lose weight, get fit or increase energy and all the usual approaches seem to fail then you need to understand more about your own uniqueness. I would always recommend strongly that everyone see their doctor to make sure there is no underlying health problem and oversee any changes in your health regime. Fatigue and weight gain can be symptoms of health conditions such as diabetes or under-active thyroid which need to be treated appropriately. If you have been there, done that to no avail then there could be a hidden imbalance that is individual to you.

Is there a hidden imbalance?

If there is an imbalance weight is often just a symptom of that imbalance other common symptoms of an imbalance:

- Fatigue?
- Dry, blotchy skin?
- Digestive aches and pains?
- Urinary problems, mood fluctuations?

The biggest clue - Any chronic condition that has failed to respond to treatment. 10 is the average number of years people live with a condition before they find out they have a food intolerance.

FOOD FOR LIFE

Why No Weight Loss?

As you can see balance is vital for health and well-being and our relationship with food is probably the most important balancing act. What you put into your body has a huge effect on its ability to function, manage and maintain. We all know we need food and water to survive but it can't be just any old food or fluid if you also want to stay fit and healthy. Your body has thousands of different components that need constant maintenance and a vast array of tasks to carry out and this requires a quantity and variety of nutrients. The choice is simple, you either put in the things that make you look and feel good, or you don't. We usually recognise the importance of food as an energy source but forget it also provides the building blocks of life, your life in fact. Your entire body structure and functions are built, maintained and run predominately from the nutrients you obtain from food.

In the past we have always associated malnourishment with starvation. In today's society there is a new phenomena, people are suffering from being both undernourished and overweight. For many their basic relationship with food has gone bad, diets are undernourished, unvaried and unbalanced leaving the body weak and less able to cope with normal everyday demands.

Why a varied diet...

Like a jigsaw puzzle there are loads of different pieces that all need to interlock to complete your daily essential nutritional requirements. One missing bit and the job remains unfinished.

Why a balanced diet...

No one food item contains all the nutrients you need. Eating lots of one type of food and neglecting others is nutritionally pointless. Nutrients and fluids rarely work independently they usually need other elements to enable them to do their job. Eating the same foods over and over again will also deprive your body of other essential nutrients from other foods. Oversupply means the body has to find somewhere to store or dispose of the excess unused, adding additional storage and waste removal problems.

If you think you follow a healthy diet but still have weight and health problems then it is important to re-examine your diet regardless of whether or not you think it is healthy.

FOOD OVERLOAD

Forget about classifying foods as good or bad the real route to nutritional and weight imbalance is too much or too little for too long. If you class something as good then, theoretically, the more you eat, the healthier you become. Bad on the other hand is sinful and needs to be avoided at all costs. All you despairing dieters out there will be reassured to know that a diet of nothing but fruit and salad is unadvisable long-term because fruit is very high in sugar, salad has little nutritional value and the whole thing is nutritionally unbalanced. A diet like this may initially seem a good idea for weight loss but it is neither sustainable, healthy or enjoyable long-term. With all food there is a pay off, some of its components are good but others are either of no value or potentially harmful in large

Is your diet really healthy?

- Do you double eat? Basically you fancy chips, have a salad instead then eat chips later anyway
- Eat something healthy but nick food of someone else's plate?
- Do you take any notice of what you are eating when you are eating?
- Are you in denial? Do you ignore alcohol intake or picking?
- How much of a meal do you actually taste? Every mouthful or none at all?
- Do you know what an average portion size is?
- Do you not include holidays and special occasions in a healthy eating plan?

Why No Weight Loss?

quantities. For example milk is an excellent source of calcium but high in fat and its complex make-up can make digestion difficult putting it in the top ten food intolerances. Psychologically the good and bad food mindset makes it much harder to eat healthy or maintain a balanced weight. Before you have even eaten them, good foods are perceived dull and unsatisfying and bad foods are naughty and therefore must be pleasurable because they are to be indulged. Yes some foods are better to eat than others because they have a much higher nutritional density or ratio but a balanced diet accounts for all your requirements in the right quantities so you shouldn't feel deprived, should enjoy and still maintain a healthy weight.

Nutritional density

Nutritional density describes the amount of nutrients in an individual food item. Nuts for example have a high nutritional density because per 100 grams they have an extremely dense nutritional content. Where as lettuce has a very low nutritional content as it is 98% water.

Nutritional ratio

Nutritional ratio is when a food item or more appropriately a meal has a balance of nutrients that correspond with healthy eating guidelines. So for example, it has the right percentage of fat, protein and carbohydrate to make it balanced nutritionally.

Are you a good/bad food selector?

- Do you go for diets that promise big weight loss or prefer to just generally eat more healthy?
- Do you rate food as good and bad just by their calorie content?
- Do you avoid nuts and seeds because they are high in fat and calories but have a cream cake as a treat?
- Write down all the foods you think are good and all the foods you think are bad - why do you think they are good or bad?
- Do you class all your good foods as boring and your bad foods as foods you would eat all the time if you didn't have to worry about your weight?

Generally in a balanced diet so called bad foods such as chocolate and red wine are perfectly good. On the other hand a diet of nothing but chocolate and red wine is not good which is why balance is so important but you also have to consider your own individual needs. For example if you are lactose-intolerant then there is no benefit in drinking milk no matter what nutritional benefits it may contain. In this case the problem is detectable but in many cases finding out what suits you personally is more instinctive. If bread blows you up like a balloon and makes you feel tired you don't bother to question why you just stop eating it but can you be sure bread is to blame and why? You could be intolerant to wheat, have a yeast or bacterial problem, have sluggish digestion, simply eating too much refined white flour or it could be something else you eat regularly and not the bread at all as negative reactions aren't always immediate. For example symptoms of food sensitivities and intolerances can take up to 72 hours to materialise. If you want to balance your weight then finding a diet that is appropriate to you personally is the key even if it takes a bit of detection work and doesn't always appear to tally with everything that is generally advised.

EATING FOR BALANCE

Very simply there are two main reasons why we need food. Firstly we need food as an energy source and secondly we need food to build and maintain body bits and make everything function internally.

MAIN SOURCES

Listed here are some main sources of each nutritional group but these only highlight the main component. Most foods contain a combination of both energy and body building nutrients but in different variations, quantities and ratios. Sugar is the most basic and simple type of food. It supplies purely for energy.

Energy comes from carbohydrates and fats

CARBOHYDRATES - Fruit, vegetables, cereals, sugar.

ENERGY FATS - Butter, margarine, cheese, milk, meat

Body building nutrients are proteins, minerals, vitamins and fats, particularly the Omega range

PROTEINS - Meat, fish, seafood, nuts, eggs, pulses

BODY BUILDING FATS – oily fish, nuts, seeds, vegetable oils, olive oil

MINERALS AND VITAMINS - meat, fish, vegetables, fruit, nuts, seeds, dairy

Basically our diet should be a combination of all these foods, but what about balance?

Here are some imbalance examples

If your diet is high in dairy produce, bread, cereal and pasta, and not much meat, fish, vegetables and nuts then your diet is too high in energy foods and too low in body building foods. Foods high in energy sources may be the obvious choice to turn to if you are feeling tired but it is the body building nutrients that enable your body to process potential energy into a usable source. So lots of potential energy may be going in but not the nutrients your body needs to process it. This does nothing to relieve your energy levels so you crave energy foods even more and it does leave your body with a problem, it now has an overload of unconverted energy nutrients so what does it do with them?

Basically it has two choices, the main one is to store this potential energy as fat until it can process it effectively and the alternative is to dispose of it as waste. The result is you will put on weight and clog your digestive system up in the process. And lets not forget you are still short of energy which means your internal systems will find it harder to cope with the additional problems of added fat and waste and you will crave more energy foods. Not only can this lead to weight gain and low energy but you are increasing your chances of developing further problems with your digestive system such as IBS and food intolerances.

Typical symptoms – food craving, low energy and bloating.

If your diet is too low in energy foods you will have no obvious energy supply so the body will have to use protein as a source of energy. This means that there will be less protein available for repair and maintenance but more tissue wasting because the protein in muscles, for example, will be stripped out. Any weight loss is going to include muscle wasting rather than fat. Also high intakes of protein amongst other things alter the natural alkaline/acidity balance and generate increased cellular damage and high levels of toxicity. This puts a real strain in particular on your kidneys and liver.

Typical symptoms – lack of stamina, poor muscle strength, bad breath and fluid retention.

If you eat lots of cakes, biscuits, chocolate and processed foods and drink lots of coffee, fizzy drinks and alcohol and you have little in the way of vegetables, meat, fish, fruit, nuts, seeds and pulses, then your diet is not just low in essential nutrients but far too high in fast-energy-release foods and stimulants. These induce immediate energy rushes followed by energy crashes. A diet like this can generate constant underlying stress on your body and cause a build up of toxins and cell damage if sustained for too long. Unfortunately you also won't have enough of the nutrients your body needs to deal with all these new problems so overtime your health will gradually decline.

Typical symptoms - massive energy and weight fluctuations, poor skin, cystitis, constipation, thrush, digestive pains and mood swings.

Energy food/body building food
Where's the imbalance?

- Typical western diets are overloaded in energy foods and low in body building foods
- Energy nutrients need body building nutrients to process energy effectively
- Lifestyle factors such as stress or lack of activity can lead to high storage of energy nutrients so more body building foods are required
- Your individual biological makeup also influences the right food ratio/balance for you

Why No Weight Loss?

IN A NUT SHELL

Eating is for life – staying at a healthy weight and keeping the shape you want is not achievable with crash diets. We need to eat healthily all the time but this doesn't mean it has to be an ordeal. You can eat lots of highly nutritious and tasty food and be happy with your body.

Weight, size and health are all influenced by the type of food we eat – we are made from the food we eat and a happy body is one that gets the resources it needs.

Balance is the key – we need the right balance of energy foods and body building foods to keep everything in balance. Weight problems are a symptom of an imbalance. This could be diet, internal, emotional or usually a mix of factors.

One imbalance leads to another – when something negative happens it has a nasty habit of generating a spiral of negative consequences that can change where the main problem lies. For example over eating may have been the initial cause of weight gain but this could have over time generated digestive disorders such as bloating, IBS or food intolerance which is maintaining the problem.

You are you – your body and the environment may be similar to others but ultimately it is unique to you. If you are struggling with weight and energy problems then sometimes general rules don't always apply.

What do you really want to sort out – weight may be your biggest complaint but are there other health and well-being issues that are really causing you grief. Perhaps it is lack of energy or control, low confidence, poor skin, fluid retention, etc.

DIGESTIVE DISORDER

How is your digestive system?

- How often do you go to the loo?
- Do you suffer from bloating?
- Do you get abdominal pain?
- Do you feel sick regularly?
- Do you suffer from heartburn?
- Is your gut painful to touch?
- Do you suffer from wind?
- Do you get constipated?

When trying to resolve weight and body shape issues, diet is the obvious first choice of exploration, the second is the digestive system. The digestive system is one of the most complex and resilient systems in the body. Not only is it a food processing centre, it has also evolved to cope with a whole array of nasties including poison, waste, toxins, bacteria, viruses and worms. It has to expose itself to the most extreme conditions, protect the rest of the body from this and offer a huge variety of functions in order to process food. For example, apparently some gut acid is strong enough to dissolve razor blades and there is over a kilo of approximately 1,000 different species of bacteria to manage. To process food it has to first break it up, separate the good from the not needed or bad, break nutrients up into individual items in order to get them distributed, dispose of any excess food and waste and remove harmful bi-products.

You might think that your skin is the natural barrier that protects you from the outside world but your digestive system also acts as an intermediate with the outside world. We need external items to survive and the digestive system is the body's immigration gateway, selecting what is safe and needed to pass into the inner workings from what is harmful or not needed. 60% of our immune defences are sited here and its tolerance level to harmful elements is generally much higher and more diverse than other internal body areas. During metabolism the body itself also produces toxic elements that also have to be disposed of and again this is the digestive system's job. Its ability to process food successfully, prevent harmful elements entering the inner workings of the body and dispose of toxic waste greatly influences our ability to manage weight and stay healthy. Likewise the more we look after it the better it will run but there is also our own individuality that dictates how well it will perform. For example, childhood diabetes and allergies both demand very specific dietary requirements that generate extra pressures on the digestive system. If you know what your weak spot is then you know you have to take additional care but there are also many more of you who are aware they may have digestive sensitivities but don't know exactly why, making them hard to manage.

Digestive problems can develop over time from negative aspects of lifestyle, such as stress and poor diet. The problem with this is that the symptoms are often vague and produce nothing diagnosable but all can potentially generate weight gain. Firstly you have the symptoms of bloating, fluid retention and inflammation to blow you up then you have the secondary problems of comfort eating and food cravings for quick fix energy foods usually high in calories and low in nutrition. Poor diet, metabolism, energy levels and nutrient adsorption can add further to the problems generating more chronic conditions such as IBS, acid reflux, diabetes and food intolerance. A dysfunctional digestive system can cause a vicious circle of problems. For example, a weak system may find it harder to process more complex foods such as wheat and dairy produce, so a food sensitivity develops. However, because you can often pinpoint the fact that these foods are generating negative symptoms, you blame it all on a food intolerance to wheat and dairy. Having excluded them from your diet, you may well experience some degree of recovery but your digestive system is still being put under strain because the original weaknesses have not been addressed. This increases the chance of you becoming more sensitive to more foods which pushes you further into a restrictive diet and lifestyle but no slimmer or more energetic.

Do you think you are sensitive?

- Do you have chronic aches and pains?
- Are there certain foods that make you feel ill?
- Do you suffer from bladder problems?
- Have you got low energy?

POWER TO YOUR GUT

So the digestive system breaks down food, extracting what it needs at various stages in the process and disposes of what it doesn't need, along with the usual collection of toxic wastes generated during metabolism but it can only do this under the right circumstances. As with everything in the body, it is a cellular structure that needs energy to power it, nutrients to repair and maintain it and time to rest in order to keep it running effectively. We tend to associate energy as something we need to move the things we can physically control like muscles and to help the brain with our thought processes. Although this is true, around two thirds of our daily energy supply is used to run all the systems in the body that we have little control over like your heart, kidneys and digestive system. If these energy requirements and nutritional resources are not met then essential processes can malfunction or be forced to slow down. You know how you feel when you are tired. You make silly mistakes, lack motivation, drop things and feel both mentally and physically weaker. If you feel tired then so will all the internal mechanisms of the body. They too will make errors, forget things and be unable to work as effectively.

The digestive system is likely to be the first system to be affected by negative factors such as an imbalance, stress or poor diet but often without any immediate or direct symptoms. This is because the digestive symptom has to process and deliver nutritional resources and energy supplies to the whole of the body, so negative symptoms can emerge elsewhere such as in the skin as supplies of energy and nutrients begin to decline as the digestive system struggles with supply.

Physical ways to see if your internal energy is too low

- Dry, flaky skin
- Skin easily bruises
- Black bags under your eyes
- Wounds take ages to heal
- Constant colds
- Mouth ulcers or cold sores
- Walk with round shoulders
- Keep your head down and frown

How do you rate your energy levels?

HIGH

LOW

INCONSISTENT

CALORIE COUNTING

Are you a calorie counter or a healthy eater?

Take an apple
- Do you know how many calories are in it?
- Is it an energy or body building food?
- Name one nutrient in it?

If you have spent a lifetime jumping from one diet to the next then you will know the calorie content but if you struggled with the other questions then you need to think more about healthy eating and less about calories.

You don't need to know the full nutritional history of food but selecting foods for their nutritional value and not calories could make the difference. If low calorie diets have failed for you perhaps it's time to change the way you view food.

When it comes to weight here's the dilemma. Our energy comes from eating calories but too many will add to our weight and put additional strain on our digestive system and too little will put us on a go slow. Everyone who watches their weight will be aware of a standard figure telling us how many calories a woman or man need. Even this varies from publication to publication but on average it is around 1600 – 2000 for women and 2200 – 2500 for a man.

Your calorie intake provides you with a calculated pot of resources that are then distributed around the body. You also have fat reserves to add to that pot which is how a calorie controlled diet works. You put less in and your body is forced to use up stored supplies. From a resources point of view, obviously essential systems come first then what is left over is for you to live your life. If there are internal imbalances more energy is used internally, leaving less for you to play with and you will feel less energetic. Even fat processing requires energy so you can see why your body hates to be put on a low calorie diet because it fears it will not have enough usable energy to go around or even process fat stores effectively. For instant energy it is much easier to go for some high calorie, sugar and fat foods that can quickly be processed. As these foods are generally so easily available with little energy expenditure, this is what your brain will ask you to do. Unfortunately these are just the kinds of foods that will stress your system out further and a vicious cycle of yo-yo dieting emerges but with little success. So if you have periods of eating too little then you will not have either the energy or nutrients to keep yourself fit and healthy and this will make it much harder to keep your weight in a balanced state.

THINGS TO REMEMBER

- Excessive or prolonged stress, coupled with unhealthy lifestyle practices and poor diet, has the same negative effects on the digestive system as anywhere else in the body.

- The digestive system is powered by muscular action so it can also suffer from musc e wasting and fatigue, slowing it down and reducing its effectiveness.

- The brain runs the digestive system and it can also be affected by low energy and nutritional supply making instructions slow and inaccurate.

- The digestive system is a cellular structure and suffers from the damaging effects of oxidation, free radicals and toxins when imbalances occur.

- With less energy systems weaken but with errors more work is created and less is done so a backlog of jobs builds up.

- Imbalances occur when a gulf emerges between the amount of work to do and the amount of resources available to do the job.

- A healthy digestive system can make it much easier to maintain a balanced weight and have the shape you want.

- And don't forget your digestive system is unique to you, it will be naturally better at some jobs than others but also you can influence the effect these imbalances can have.

EXCESS OR SENSITIVITY

Your digestive system can put up with a lot but like everything else in the body, it cannot tolerate negative extremes of anything for too long. This could be too much of the same foods, too much food, too little food, not enough nutrients, too many chemicals, too much processed or complex food, too many stimulants, too much waste, not enough fluid, too much bad bacteria, too much acid, too much irritation or too much stress.

The earlier food sensitivity example highlights the problem with "extremes." At the moment there is a big eating fad involving giving up wheat and dairy. This has happened mainly through word of mouth, and yes many have cut them out of their diet through a friendly recommendation and feel much better which for them is great. The problem is that they now assume they must be and always have been intolerant to these foods. In fact, for many it is more a case of too much for too long overloading their system. So these foods may well have been generating poor health and weight problems but this doesn't mean to say they have an intolerance to them.

Western diets are extremely high in these two food and they usually come in a highly refined and processed manner. Dietary evidence shows that as a nation we have been overeating them at the expense of other foods containing different nutrients. If you look around a supermarket and the vast array of food available it is easy to think that there is an endless choice. But if you look at the eating pattern of an average person it would be something like this:

- Cereal or toast and tea or coffee for breakfast

- Sandwich and yoghurt for lunch with a latte

- Pasta in a cream sauce with garlic bread for dinner

This may look like lots of different food items but actually the basic underlying ingredients are just wheat, dairy and caffeine. Neither wheat or dairy are "bad" foods. Wheat is a complex carbohydrate and full of fibre if it is whole grain of course and it is these two factors that make it beneficial in moderation. It takes a long time to digest, releases energy slowly and uses fibre to pick up toxic waste and dispose of it. Unfortunately in excess, especially in the more common refined form a lot of energy is used to process it, it bulks up your digestive system blowing you up like a balloon, this bulk can limit your intake of other sources of nutrition and produce more waste. For an overloaded system, this is very stressful and negative symptoms such as bloating, constipation and pain occur so its not surprising you feel better if you cut it out.

List your daily diet

- Write down everything you eat in a day such as potatoes, meat and fish and how much?
- You don't need to be too precise, just use your plate or hand to work out how much you have
- What are the basic ingredients?
- What ratio are they in?
- What makes up the majority of your diet?

The major food group in a balanced diet is vegetables - does this match your figures?

Questionnaire

- Do you eat the same foods regularly?
- Eat on the go?
- Buy ready meals?
- Snack?
- Drink more than 2 cups of coffee a day?
- Drink less than a litre of water a day?
- Drink alcohol every day?
- Smoke?
- Work long hours?

All these can influence the nutritional value of food and increase your risk of developing imbalances such as a food intolerance.

SENSITIVITY OR INTOLERANCE

Although initially your problem with certain food could be down to excess intake, if prolonged there is a possibility you could become more sensitive to them. If it is to do with pure overload then the chances of you losing weight if you cut them out is good because they are accounting for a large amount of your calorie intake. Also because of their absence in your diet you will have to introduce other foods. Your new diet will probably be more balanced and nutritious, enabling your body to function more effectively. But we shouldn't just target wheat and dairy, sensitivity could stem from a whole range of foods. I have met people who claim they eat nothing but masses of fruit, feel terrible and still have a weight problem. Often the benefit people experience as a result of giving up or cutting down on certain foods is due not only to giving their digestive system a chance to sort itself out, but because they introduce food sources that contain nutrients they had been missing out on.

Overloading your system with the same food can create a backlog of ineffectively-processed food in the gut, diminishing your ability to absorb nutrients and distribute them around the rest of the body so everything can suffer. As toxicity builds it will be harder to maintain healthy bacteria levels and slower digestive movements increase the risk of infection and harmful substances adhering to the gut wall. So how does this effect your weight?

Do any of these relate to you?

- A slow digestive system and more gas can lead to bloating.
- In a fatigued state the body is more likely to hold onto fat stores as it feels uncertain about sustained energy levels.
- Feeling tired will make you less active and motivated to do anything positive.
- Feeling miserable and out of control will encourage comfort eating.
- You are more inclined to reach for a stimulant, such as alcohol or caffeine to boost energy levels adding more chemical and toxic waste, draining it yet again.
- Food sensitivity can trigger off immune responses generating inflammation and fluid retention.

We can see that negative diet and lifestyle issues can cause sensitivity and left unchecked this could develop into a food intolerance. The problem with this is it is much harder to determine what foods you are intolerant to. We can also have individual sensitivities to certain foods even if we think we eat healthily and take care of ourselves. This is where you come into the equation. Wearing your digestive system out is one thing but it could also have always had a negative reaction or irritation to a particular food. From a food intolerance point of view what works for your friend is not necessarily going to be the same for you.

So you can either develop food intolerances from poor diet and lifestyle but you can also have always had them. The problem with this is they would have been maintaining an ongoing underlying imbalance making it harder for your digestive system to stay healthy and for you to manage your weight. Even if it only initially generated minor problems including difficulty in losing weight or maintaining stamina, any negative changes to your lifestyle including low calorie or fad dieting could generate stronger negative reactions.

How sensitive are you?

- Have you ever cut certain foods out of your diet?
- Who told you to do it?
- Did you guess?
- Did it make a difference?
- Do you think you have a food intolerance? [Go to page 114]

How happy is your gut?

Are you happy with -

- Your weight and body shape?
- How much energy you have?
- Your confidence levels?
- Your mood?

BRING IN THE BACTERIA

- Bacteria make up most of the flora in the colon and 60% of faeces

- Between 400 and 1000 different species live in the gut but 99% come from approximately 35 species

- Bacteria are responsible for the production of vitamin B12, vital for cell division, blood formation and energy production. Animals eat the bacteria and then when we eat the meat, eggs or milk we get the vitamin

Whether your imbalances stem from lifestyle, diet, individual imbalances or more likely a mix, if left unchecked they could destabilize the delicately balanced internal environment of the gut. Digestion and waste management involve a complex range of processes involving enzymes and hormones, acids and alkaline and a large colony of bacteria.

It is weird to think we have trillions of little organisms living in their own world inside our colon but the type and level of bacteria in our gut can dictate how well it functions. Emerging research is now showing it could now also influence our ability to gain and lose weight. As with food the term good and bad bacteria is often used but it is of course not as simple as that. Firstly bacteria, although essential in aiding digestion and absorption in the gut is not necessarily good for the rest of the body. The gut has to contain and manage them in a confined area. So they are good where they are but not so good if they go elsewhere. Secondly, it is, as always about balance, too much or too little of certain kinds of gut bacteria can generate gut problems including bloating and weight gain.

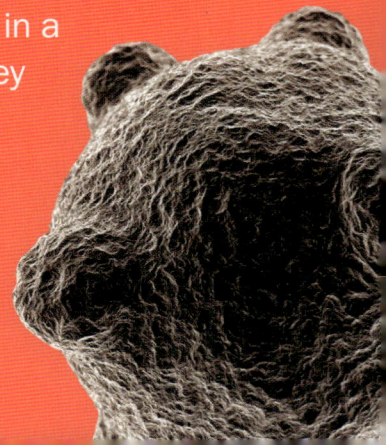

Why No Weight Loss?

What healthy bacteria do

Utilize carbohydrates – some bacteria have specific enzymes for breaking down starch, fibre and sugars. Without these we wouldn't be able to digest them successfully. They can also absorb and dispose of alcohols, mucus and excess proteins as too much protein can be toxic.

Increase the gut's absorption of water – one of the biggest problems of dehydration in the gut is constipation but water is essential for many more gut processes.

Produce organic acids – during carbohydrate fermentation acids are produced including propionic acid that helps in the production of energy and acetic acid, used by the muscles.

Stimulate new cells – bacteria increase and control the growth of healthy new cells in the gut and help protect them from harm. Short chain fatty acids produced by gut bacteria also provide fuel for intestinal cells.

Preventing the growth of harmful micro-organisms – compare the gut wall to the most expensive bit of real estate, there is a constant fight to find a place to stop and establish yourself. A gut full of good bacteria will mean there will be no room left for harmful organisms such as viruses and yeast to stay. They also compete for nutrition, starving harmful invaders of energy and food. Gut bacteria also produce substances designed to kill harmful microbes and act as a decoy so that the invader will stick to them and not the gut wall.

Enhance the immune system – in our early development, healthy bacteria help define our gut immunity and then continues to play a key role all through life. Bacteria help produce antibodies, important in the fight against pathogens and desensitizes allergic and intolerance related immune responses. They can also assist the immune system in the repair of damaged tissue and have antibiotic properties.

Disease defences – healthy bacteria can help reduce the incidence of certain gut related diseases such as Crohn's and help reduce inflammation. Recent research by the University College London showed a link between Irritable Bowel Disease and raised levels of the IgG antigen, the antigen associated with food intolerance that bacteria help to de-sensitize. A healthy intestinal ecosystem also protects against infections such as E.Coli and protects the gut against the toxic effects of drugs used

What is the difference between a pre and probiotic?

- Probiotics are bacteria beneficial to the gut
- Prebiotics are the food they eat which we provide for them in our diet
- Prebiotics are found in vegetables and fruit

to combat disease. New research is now highlighting a possible link between bacterial balance and protection against certain cancers.

Disease defences – healthy bacteria can help reduce the incidence of certain gut related diseases such as Crohn's and help reduce inflammation. Recent research by the UCL showed a link between Irritable Bowel Disease and raised levels of the IgG antigen, the antigen associated with food intolerance that bacteria help to de-sensitize. A healthy intestinal ecosystem also protects against infections such as E.Coli and protects the gut against the toxic effects of drugs used to combat disease. New research is now highlighting a possible link between bacterial balance and protection against certain cancers.

Produce body building nutrients – bacteria produce and help the body absorb vitamins like vitamin K, some B vitamins and minerals such as calcium, magnesium and iron.

Maintain a healthy pH – healthy bacteria keep the pH low in the gut preventing the growth of harmful species who thrive on higher pH. Lower pH is also believed to increase the excretion of harmful substances.

Help develop the gut – your gut flora is unique to you. Our levels and range of bacteria vary as it is formulated after birth and this can then dictate how well the gut and immune system works. Bacteria are associated with the prevention of allergies or over-sensitized immune reactions as it helps train the immune system at an early age. Known as oral tolerance, bacteria can reduce the sensitivity of an auto-immune response. The fluctuating health of our gut through life also dictates how well we do or don't respond to negative exposure.

Cut down on bloating and gas – harmful bacteria and yeast create gas as a bi-product and generate bloating. A healthy gut flora keeps things moving and cuts down the embarrassing effects of the build up and release of gas.

One of the most interesting lines of research happening at the moment is the relationship between our own individual gut flora and our ability to utilize calories and store fat. What we eat and how we live our life seems to greatly influence what types and what level of healthy bacteria our gut contains. New research in America has indicated that a diet high in refined carbohydrates and fats could change the ratio of certain bacteria, the ones good at breaking up these specific carbohydrates. Unfortunately these are also the most efficient at extracting calories and encouraging fat storage. They are also indicating a link between obesity and individual differences in gut bacteria. Obese individuals could have more of these specific bacteria, unfortunately also associated with converting waste into methane gas, making you not just bigger but more noticeable!

Further research has linked the effectiveness of bacteria to process more calories and store more fat with the hormone Leptin. Low levels put the brain into starvation mode and this appears to trigger signals aimed at the bacteria to become more efficient at collecting calories and encouraging fat production.

Fortunately work carried out over the last 12 years in this country by Professor Glen Gibson has demonstrated our ability to manipulate our own gut flora to our advantage mainly through eating a diet high in Prebiotics, found predominately in fruit and vegetables such as bananas and onions. Prebiotics are basically the food healthy bacteria thrive off enabling them to flourish while unhealthy bacteria and yeast are left to starve.

In a healthy gut, the number of harmful bacteria is controlled at a safe level, allowing the beneficial bacteria to get on with the job of keeping the digestive tract healthy. However ongoing imbalances can allow bacteria to multiply excessively in the gut.

What pushes the gut out of balance?

- Nutritionally poor and unbalanced diet
- A high intake of alcohol, refined and processed food, sugar and fat
- Antibiotics
- Stress
- Low energy and poor health smoking

How our gut can be imbalanced?

- Unrecognized food intolerance or sensitivity
- The strength of our unique bacterial ecosystem
- Hormones
- Acid/alkaline irregularities
- Sluggish digestion
- Low metabolism

What happens when bacteria go bad
a cycle of destruction

- Colonies of yeasts and harmful bacteria overgrow pushing down levels of healthy bacteria further. In a healthy environment yeast normally live on dead tissue. The most commonly known yeast, Candida if left to spread will start to feast on healthy living tissue in the gut.

- Other invaders such as Helicobactor Pylori will also burrow into the gut wall generating further damage and inflammation.

- This puts extra pressure on the immune system but its effectiveness is depleted due to the loss of the healthy bacteria which usually assists it.

- Nutritional processing and absorption will be diminished making it harder to maintain health.

- All this can dramatically drain energy levels.

- The brain switches to stress mode, suppressing the immune system and calling for high energy foods, blood sugar levels rise and hormones enhance the absorption and storage of fat.

- Problems with food processing and immunity can lead to food intolerance.

- Bloating, fluid retention and inflammation start to cause swelling.

- You feel fat, fed-up and out of control.

LEAKY GUT – FACT OR FICTION

The theory of leaky gut is that when the gut wall gets too permeable, acids, bacteria, yeast, pathogens and unprocessed food particles can then spread into the rest of the body causing a whole catalogue of harm. It is claimed that harmful bacteria and yeast can pass through the gut wall through a process called translocation. This translocation activates the immune system resulting in inflammation in the gut wall, damaging the protective barrier further. If they pass the gut defensive barrier and reach the blood stream, infections can occur throughout the body. Further immune responses at the site of infection result in more inflammation and so it goes on.

From a scientific point of view leaky gut is still to be fully established but there does appear to be a growing band of evidence to suggest that it could explain some of the vague but unpleasant chronic health issues many seem to experience today. We have already seen how an unhappy gut can add to weight and body shape issues so imagine the impact if the imbalances spread further.

Science is still debating on leaky gut but then 10 years ago the majority of us knew very little about gut flora or food intolerance. Usually when a growing band of public find something that works for them that is when science really starts its research. But biologically we know that the gut wall can be damaged and made more permeable so the theory is not fantastical just needs further investigation to explain the consequences more fully.

HOW DOES IT HAPPEN

Symptoms often associated with leaky gut

- Thrush
- Cystitis
- Fatigue
- Cramps
- Bloating

What's this got to do with weight?

- Fluid retention
- Areas of fat, fluid and toxins
- Bloating
- Inflammation
- Increase in fat storage
- Food craving for sugar, fat and carbs
- You feel fed up and comfort eat

- All gut walls are meant to be permeable but there are reasons why some may be more permeable than others.

- Yeast and harmful bacteria damage.

- Weakness in the cells through lack of energy or nutrition.

- Damage from the effects of stress, chemicals such as smoking, injury or infection.

- Swelling and inflammation from the immune response attacking the wall to fight a pathogen.

- The effects of an inappropriate immune response to a food allergy or intolerance.

- Excess acid.

- Your genetic make-up.

- How your gut and immune system matured.

As usual there is no one thing but more a collection of negative elements happening together but basically you can separate these into two categories

1. **Negative lifestyle factors** – the usual suspects I am afraid, diet, smoking, stress, alcohol, you name it most of us have tried it.

2. **Your personal biology** – things unique to you that make you more vulnerable to gut problems such as sluggish gut metabolism, poor blood sugar management or food intolerance.

HOW IT WORKS

We know that when we eat we have to allow external substances to pass into the internal world of the body otherwise we starve. However, the pay off is we also have to ingest potentially harmful elements that come as part and parcel of the food. The gut is therefore heavily guarded by the immune system and protected by a strong cellular wall. Although the gut wall needs to be a very strong protective barrier it also has to be permeable to allow essential nutrients in. So the gut has evolved to only allow particles below a certain size to pass through the wall. As most bacteria or viruses are bigger than the average nutrient making a net with holes small enough to catch harmful stuff but big enough to let essential nutrients through is a great idea but it does mean that food has to be broken down into the most basic molecules. Powerful acids, mechanical churning and bacteria fermentation are some of the ways that have had to be devised to enable this to happen in the gut. Again a great idea but many of the components involved in these processes such as bacteria and acid also need to be contained in specific areas to prevent harm.

As added protection immune cells are posted around the gut wall just in case anything harmful does pass through. The immune response also has the same system of recognition, to only respond to unrecognized particles over a certain size otherwise it would react to nutrients or every little tiny thing that sneaked in. So small individual nutritional components can pass through safely and the odd harmful substance but if a group of harmful elements or even a partially processed clump of nutrients managed to pass through the immune system would start to take an interest. Immune cells also have many other forms of recognition such as levels of stickyness and antibody recognition but the size thing initially generally works very well if the system is healthy, the gut wall is strong and does not have any in-built faults.

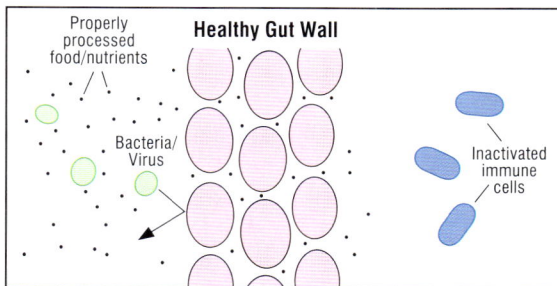

Healthy Gut Wall

Properly processed food/nutrients
Bacteria/Virus
Inactivated immune cells

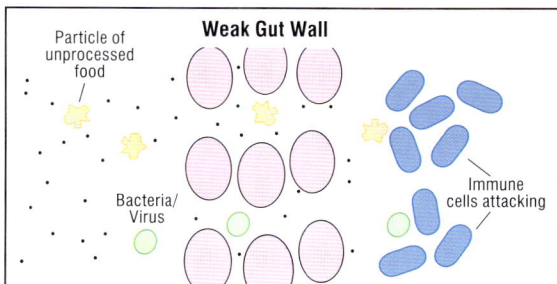

Weak Gut Wall

Particle of unprocessed food
Bacteria/Virus
Immune cells attacking

GUT FACTS WE FORGET

- A healthy digestive system processes food and separates the waste from the essential nutrients generating maximum nutrients and minimal waste.

- It disposes of food waste, toxins and other waste products produced naturally from other internal body functions and any junk we expose ourselves to.

- It absorbs nutrients and feeds the rest of the body with all the essential components it requires for repair, growth, maintenance and effective functioning, greatly influencing health.

- We have no voluntary control over most of the digestive processing or the internal systems it supplies but a large percentage of our energy and resources are used to run them.

- The digestive and immune systems work very closely to maintain health and balance in the rest of the body so a problem with one can affect the other.

- Because our digestive system is so good at doing its job we often forget it actually needs our help. We are the only ones that can give it the right food, fluid and create the right emotional balance – the gut hates stress and unhappiness.

- Your digestive system is unique to you. In all of us the process is technically the same but each one of us will have differences in the way we absorb certain nutrients, dispose of waste, balance bacteria or trigger an immune response and all this has an influence on what size and shape we are.

Get to know your gut

- **What does it feel like after you have eaten?** – in the morning? – when you go to bed? -does it rumble? - feel sore, painful?

- **Are you considerably heavier in the evening?** get a bad taste in your mouth? - have bad breath? - burp lots?

WORKING WITH YOUR WEAKNESSES

Remember the two key elements of an imbalance are lifestyle and personal biology. With weight it is easy to understand that if you eat too much fatty, sugary foods, never exercise and feel miserable you are more likely to have weight problems but it can be much harder to relate your weight to individual differences. We can all understand that if biologically we are shorter in height than other people, basketball is not going to be a good sport to excel at because we can visualise it. When it comes to internal differences most are microscopic and even if they were not you couldn't see them anyway which is why they can be so difficult to detect.

When we know we have strengths and weaknesses we put our energies into our strengths and adapt to our weaknesses enabling us to live a happy and healthy life. This is much harder if you don't know what they are. If you are fit and healthy then they will probably not be a problem but if you feel tired, fed-up and over weight and can't seem to get to grips with it then small individual imbalances can make a difference. Negative lifestyle factors such as too much stress or poor diet can highlight a weakness or even generate a new one and once the imbalance is in place this can maintain a problem even if you make attempts to improve your diet and lifestyle.

What triggered off your weight problems?

- Has it got worse with age?
- Bout of illness?
- Relationship breakdown?
- Job loss?
- Any other negative factors?

GUT HAPPINESS

Before you can recognise what works for you we first need to look at what's not good for your digestive system. Generally any negative imbalance will put pressure on the gut meaning it has to work much harder just to achieve basic targets such as processing food and supplying the body with resources. If the gut is under-resourced and under-strain then it may fail to reach these targets generating a vicious circle of decline. Reduced resource leads to reduced ability. This leads to inefficient processing, more waste, more work which means more resources when less are available because they aren't there or are not being fully processed. This cycle generates a slow decline in the health and wellbeing of not just the digestive system but the entire body making it less able to cope. Ability falls further and a wide gap emerges between the amount of energy and resources needed to keep things balanced and healthy and what is actually available.

WHEN THE GUT IS UNHAPPY

The whole digestive system slows down – The constant movement of the gut not only keeps nutritional supplies going but also removes waste quickly and reduces the chances of infection as bugs don't get an opportunity to colonise.

Absorption is reduced – Poor processing means less food is broken down into individual nutritional components. Theoretically in a sluggish gut you will need to eat more food to get all the nutrients you need.

More waste is generated – The gut has to separate the stuff it wants from the stuff it doesn't and this can be anything from bacteria found on the food to toxic substances within it. When the body comes to absorb the nutrients anything stuck to them will mean they will either not pass through the gut wall or become detectable to the immune system. Either way everything will be rejected and disposed of as waste and you will feel bunged up and bloated.

Cells weaken – The gut is a cellular structure which is constantly being repaired and maintained. Every cell needs nutrients and energy and a decline in either makes them more vulnerable to disease and damage and more likely to weaken, malfunction and shrink. This is basically what the leaky gut theory suggests as the gut wall thins it becomes more permeable enabling larger more harmful molecules to pass through, triggering off an immune response.

The immune system becomes more sensitive – By the time nutrients reach the point of absorption they should be individual components but poor processing can mean that more clumps of partially processed nutrients will be found further down the gut where they shouldn't be. In this scenario in the development of food intolerances it is believed to be the partially processed food proteins that generate the inflammation as the immune response will not recognise them and see these as harmful invaders. The immune response then registers this make up of proteins in its "harmful to the body" memory bank leading to repeat a response every time that food is eaten.

Yeast grows – In a healthy gut yeast is present but is maintained at a safe level. In an unhealthy gut however, yeast can colonise easily. Yeast is opportunistic and once established can do real damage to the gut wall in its need to expand. It has powerful hooks that tear through tissue and it can even alter the DNA in digestive cells to include yeast DNA so that when new cells try to replace themselves, yeast will grow with it.

Bloating and fluid retention increase – Part of the essential natural process of the immune response is to generate swelling and produce inflammation. More fluid is retained in the area effected as cells swell.

Leaves the body vulnerable to attack – A problem involves more effort, resources and energy which have to be diverted from elsewhere in the body but even then the immune response has only limited supplies leaving other areas with less protection from harmful bugs and bacteria.

All systems come under pressure – Ongoing immune responses also cause damage to the cells in the gut wall as inflammation and toxins produced by the immune response add to the problem of permeability and strength. Other areas of the body can also be negatively affected by these immune reactions generating further imbalances.

- Unhealthy gut

- Can upset blood sugar levels

- Trigger off a stress response – greater demand for energy so crave foods

- Over-sensitize immune system and generate a food intolerance

- Lethargy and pain - less active

- Leave you feeling miserable – comfort eat

ANY FOOD WILL DO IT

Why would a food intolerance affect my weight?

- Inflammatory response can lead to fluid retention and bloating

- A body under stress is more likely to store fat and unbalance blood sugar levels

- Food has a comfort factor and pain relieving properties

- Become less active as energy levels fall

- Higher demand for energy foods as immune responses are constantly activated

- You feel less social, more miserable and hate the way you look

Once again we can see the connection between lifestyle and individual differences. Food intolerances could occur from an in-built genetic fault or because the gut is not functioning to its full capacity. A sluggish gut could be because of negative lifestyle practices or it could be because of an in-built imbalance, both influence each other. The good news is if a food sensitivity or intolerance has developed through a digestive disorder then this does mean there is a chance you can reverse the process. By temporarily eliminating the offending foods and taking steps to improve overall gut health, this could restore the digestive balance, processing will improve and the chances of an intolerant reaction will reduce. The problem is that the foods generating the reaction are not the same to everyone. There are certain foods like wheat and dairy that have a higher probability of generating a reaction but this is definitely not always the case and the mix of foods can vary from person to person. So if we want to address this issue we need to look at lifestyle and dietary changes that are both good for general heath and for you individually.

INTOLERANCE INDICATORS

Can't shift condition - Symptoms of an intolerance can be quite vague or minor but they are usually chronic so low energy, weight that is difficult to lose, constant bloating or mood swings can be a sign.

Quick fix food cravings – To boost mood and energy the body can resort to desperate, immediate quick fix solutions. Food high in immediate energy sources are usually high in calories and carbs. Although they may give immediate relief, long-term they add to the problem. If you have fat then you have energy but it takes more effort to process stored fat than it does to get glucose from a food source high in pure sugar or fat. Unfortunately you also gain weight and feel out of control with your eating.

Stimulant junkie – Alcohol, smoking and caffeine all boost energy and mood temporarily by triggering off a mini adrenaline rush but constant consumption can have negative long-term consequences. Alcohol is often disregarded in healthy eating plans because it is not food but it is high in calories and not much else. The other two may not have any calories but they contain toxic chemicals that drain energy levels and block the action of certain nutrients. You know this and try to cut down but your body needs that energy boost and keeps the craving going, you on the other hand won't take kindly to the fluid retention and low energy.

Feel bloated – Complex carbohydrates are normally recommended in a healthy eating plan but many people find they feel bloated after eating them. This does not necessarily mean they are intolerant to them but could be a sign they have a digestive imbalance or even an intolerance to another food. It takes longer for the digestive system to process complex carbs which in a healthy system is good because it gives you a constant slow release of energy but a sluggish digestive system leads to poor processing and complex foods involve a lot of that.

Get ill or take ages to heal wounds – If your immune system is constantly having inappropriate reactions to foods it will be over worked and under-resourced. It will be less able to cope with all the usual bugs and things it gets exposed to on a daily basis.

Moody and irritable – Constant irritation and inflammation is not going to help your mood especially when you can't pinpoint the cause. If your body is unhappy about something it is going to let you know by sending out negative symptoms to indicate something is wrong. When efforts to lose weight fail for no apparent reason, lack of control and a sense of failure will make it harder to cope with stress or keep your self esteem up. You may be wondering what this has got to do with the digestive system but if you feel emotionally and physically less able to cope, then so will your gut.

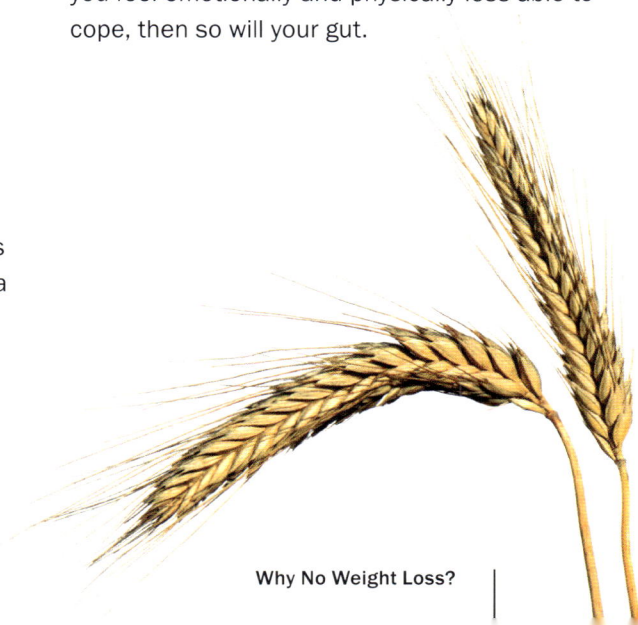

THE FI LINK WITH WEIGHT

A food intolerance is an inappropriate unhealthy reaction to a specific food that normally should cause no threat to health at all. Recent research has indicated a link between food intolerance and a range of well known but often hard to treat chronic conditions such as IBS, ME, migraine, skin problems and irritable bladder. With such an array of conditions to study the general ongoing problem with weight and the general feeling of "unwellness" that so many of us seem to complain of today was not considered until data collected from food intolerance sufferers started to show a pattern. When food intolerances were addressed for a range of conditions, two of the fortunate side effects seemed to be weight normalization and increased energy. In fact over half the people questioned in a recent study said their weight had changed for the better just by cutting out the foods they were intolerant to. If they also followed a healthy eating plan the chances are that this statistic would improve dramatically.

The theory behind FI and weight loss

Research is in its infancy but these are some of the theories suggested

- Identifying your intolerances stops inappropriate immune responses generating swelling and inflammation
- Blood sugar levels become more stable
- Energy levels increase
- Your diet may become healthier and more balanced
- You eat less calories
- You feel more active and do other things rather than eat
- You learn more about food
- You feel more in control and less stressed
- Bloating and fluid retention decline
- As with most things in the body it is probably a combination of things that include both biological reactions and how you then react to that

THE FI DEBATE

- Suffered an allergic reaction as a child
- Get hay fever, eczema, headaches, or other allergy related condition
- Have had long standing health issues such as cystitis or IBS
- You think you eat healthy food but never seem to lose weight
- Your problem started after a bout of ill health
- You constantly have low levels of energy

We still have a lot to learn about food intolerance and there is a great deal of confusion surrounding it. Firstly there is an ongoing debate about what comes under a food intolerance umbrella.

This is further complicated by the fact that scientifically they are more likely to be referred to as a delayed allergy. More generally, food intolerance can also come under a much wider food sensitivity heading.

There are also multiple reasons why the body can inappropriately react to food. With a conventional allergy, reactions are immediate and generally isolated from other biological and environmental influences. It is true to say that other factors can increase the severity of an allergic reaction but generally speaking you will always get them no matter how old, fit, healthy or stressed out you are. Health problems stem from individual food items triggering a well recognised IgE immune response and if the offending item is eliminated from the diet symptoms stop allowing the sufferer to lead a full and healthy life. With food intolerance there are different biological explanations most commonly involving enzymes or IgG antibodies. If you combine this with the fact that these biological processes occur in varying and fluctuating degrees under different conditions such as dietary, environmental, genetic, stress, health status and age, its no surprise that pinpointing and pigeonholing food intolerances into neat little boxes is virtually impossible. This dynamic interrelation and integration of factors can produce a reaction when none has knowingly ever existed before, trigger and maintain chronic conditions, aggravate other health conditions and negatively contribute to more lifestyle related conditions such as weight management.

DELAYS AND DETECTION

If we look again at a classical allergy, the symptoms are immediate and often quite severe, sometimes life threatening. Even if there were no scientific evidence it would be hard not to reach a pretty quick conclusion about what was triggering such severe reactions because the evidence is right there. Often advancements in medical research come from first knowing that something harmful happens and then looking for a scientific explanation behind it. Because food allergy reactions are in many cases so obvious, it has been easier to study and locate the cause. With food intolerance, symptoms are more delayed, less severe, not life threatening and not specific so it is much easier to get them mixed up with other health conditions. To make it even more vague, the symptoms are often tied up with other health conditions because if you have a chronic condition such as IBS or fatigue this could also be aggravated by for example, stress or poor diet. Unfortunately poor lifestyle and dietary habits can also encourage food intolerance reactions so it is not difficult to see how hard it is to unravel the real reasons behind the symptoms as it may not be just one thing. Another difference between allergies and intolerances that make them harder to detect is due to the fact that the IgE antibodies involved in a classical allergy are usually found in surface tissue such as in the skin or mouth, with food intolerance the offending food has to go through the digestive process before it produces a reaction and as individual food vary in processing times this can be anything from 30 minutes to 3 days, hence the fluctuating delay in reactions. Also with classical allergies even a micro amount can trigger a reaction where as food intolerances are more dose dependent so offending foods usually need to be eaten regularly and in quantity to produce some sort of reaction. From a general health point of view, food eaten to excess over a prolonged time period is not healthy as this not only leads to nutritional imbalances. An excess can also increase the risk of developing digestive disorders and a food intolerance so it is more of a chicken and egg scenario than finding a direct cause and isolating it.

Differences between food allergy and intolerance

- Allergy reactions are immediate, usually only one food, can be life threatening, affect skin and airways, are permanent, your lifestyle or state of health has little influence

- IgE antibodies are responsible for allergies

- Food intolerance reactions can take days, involve multiple foods, affect any bodily system, can be acquired or overcome, lifestyle and state of health is very influential

- IgG antibodies and enzymes are most commonly associated with food intolerance

FI UNDERCOVER

Do you refer to food as your "props" and the "only thing that keeps me going."

Another difficulty with detection stems from the fact that the foods that are creating the problem are often those you enjoy or eat the most. If you eat a lot of the same foods, this increases the chance of a reaction to them. With some food intolerances, we can feel good after eating them, even though long term they are making us feel awful. This initial positive reaction called "masking" can encourage us to eat even more of the same increasing our chances of greater sensitivity.

It can be difficult to accept that a "feel good" food is the cause of our problem and to make it even harder there could well be an initial adverse reaction when the food is eliminated from our diet.

There are many theories as to why the body would want to enjoy something that is so harmful to it but the body has a very strong survival mechanism that is activated when it feels under threat. The priority becomes short term coping rather than long term health maintenance. If we look at other things that have the same "masking" effect, such as stimulants like caffeine, nicotine, alcohol and foods high in fat, salt and sugar, they all have a similar effect on the body. We use them as quick fixes to keep us going when we are busy or to put us in a more positive mood. Even though we know they could be detrimental to our health and make us feel worse in the long run, we often become completely addicted to them because of that short initial burst of pleasure and stimulation they provide.

Generating an immune response can trigger the body into survival mode. This is controlled by the stress response which also provides us with pleasure and stimulation. Take smoking for example, this triggers off the stress response because you have just unbalanced the body by filling it full of potentially life threatening chemicals.

What food stimulates you?

Top 5 stimulants

- Chocolate
- Cheese
- Coffee
- Salted peanuts
- Cake and biscuits

Replace them with foods that give you a natural healthy high

- Nuts
- Seeds
- Fruit
- Porridge
- Roasted vegetables

This puts the body on red alert and stimulates it into action. It is this stimulating effect of the stress response releasing Adrenaline into the body that we find so exciting because it will immediately fill us with energy. When the stress response is activated, you will get an adrenaline rush that instigates anti-inflammatory and pain-killing forces which initially feels like a good thing. We all know of situations for example, where people have broken a bone during an activity and carried on their task with no unpleasant sensations only to discover the severity of the injury when they have finished.

This is known as masking and even though this feel-good factor is short-lived and the long-term negative symptoms soon kick in, it is still enough to give you a small window of relief. In the case of a food intolerance, this then encourages you to continue eating the offending food, your system is never free of it and more ongoing inflammation will be produced. Like going on a low calorie diet, removing something like foods high in sugar or fat that triggers off stimulating responses leaves the body feeling initially deprived because these have become a habitual prop to keep you going.

Let's not also forget that food generally has a stimulating effect, it is the body's way of getting you to put in all the essential nutrients it requires to survive. Imagine if we received no pleasure from food the human species would have starved itself out of existence thousands of years ago. Unfortunately the higher the calories, fat and sugar content the more likely we are to love and crave it because it didn't used to be so easy to get our hands on it. So once again we can see how lifestyle and individual biology interrelate to determine what does and doesn't suit you.

THE IMMUNE RESPONSE SIMPLY EXPLAINED

The immune system is designed to protect the body from harm and acts with military precision when it is up to the job. The body is constantly being bombarded with potentially harmful bacteria, viruses and substances from the environment. We also have to put things into our body to survive. Although these substances have beneficial elements, they could also contain or carry elements that could be potentially harmful to the body. Even the healthy elements could be harmful if they are not processed effectively or in excess so the immune response is constantly on guard.

The aim of the immune response is to deal with any potentially harmful substance before it can become harmful to the body. With a strong, healthy immune system, it deals with these elements without us even being aware that there is a problem. It does try to avoid conflict but if it feels there is a potential threat, if a minor problem persists or grows in strength its actions can be rapid and ruthless. As with any war, if things get desperate it will resort to chemical or biological weaponry and if all else fails, just blow everything up including its own cells.

One of the immune systems first line of internal defence is through the ability to inflate cells. Cells activated by the immune response will surround the offending molecule such as a virus, food protein or bacteria, referred to as an antigen. The cells will then blow up like a big rubber dingy. This action is designed to isolate the antigen, stop it travelling, multiplying or spreading and protect surrounding cells, allowing the rest of the body to function normally. Unfortunately it can also lead to discomfort, inflammation and swelling.

Once the antigen is contained the immune response will send a variety of specialist immune cells into the problem area to eradicate the offending item.

Why No Weight Loss?

There are a variety of specialist immune cells available, all with different functions. Some will help to advertise the location of the antigen, some will round antigens up, engulf or inactivate it, some literally eat the antigen then blow themselves up or use powerful chemicals to dissolve everything within it.

A healthy immune system is fast and effective at dealing with problems and quick at disposing of the remains. Unfortunately some of the affects of the immune response can be unpleasant. Like all war zones there will be an area of devastation once the battle is over.

Surrounding areas in the body can be affected by the fallout and damage from the actions of the immune cells. Although the immune system will mop up the remains left over from the battle, it will leave behind a damaged area for the body to repair, swelling and exhaustion.

As well as destruction, the immune system also has a memory bank. In this it will register a list of all the antigens it will have come across. This list is constantly updated as the health, experience and environment of the body changes. If a specific antigen appears again then the immune system will know immediately if it is something that needs to be attacked.

With a food intolerance, once the immune system has responded to a certain food, then that food will now be registered into the memory bank of the immune system. From then on, every time that food enters the digestive system, there will be an immune response against it.

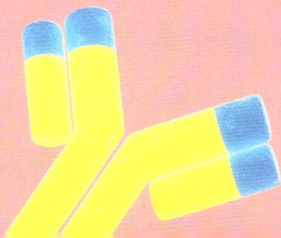

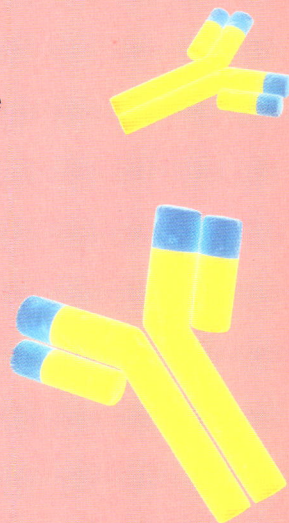

1 Unprocessed food particle

IgG antibody

Food particle

2 IgG antibody recognises and attaches to it

3 Alerts immune cell

Immune cell

4 Immune cell engulfs particle

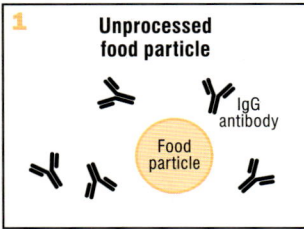

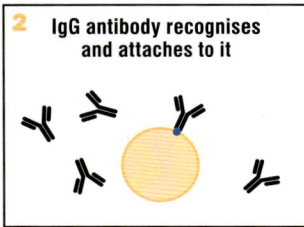

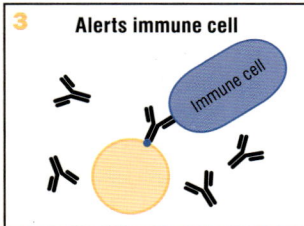

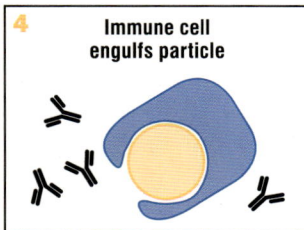

FOOD REACTIONS AND THE IMMUNE RESPONSE

Normally the immune system does not react to food. This is because it should have been trained to ignore it and because properly processed nutrients are too small to be noticed.

With a healthy gut wall, these are the main items allowed to pass through as they are the only thing small enough. Larger, unprocessed molecules will pass through the whole digestive tract and be excreted as waste.

There are a number of different causes of food intolerance but the most common is an IgG immune reaction and the key element in food that generates this reaction is the protein.

This definitely does not mean that proteins are bad or should be excluded in the diet, in fact this would be virtually impossible anyway as nearly every food source contains protein and it is vital for body repair and maintenance. In fact even the immune system depends on proteins to function. The only food that does not contain any protein is sugar which we know is very unhealthy in excess which is why you can never consider food intolerance in isolation as there are other reasons why food can be a problem.

Proteins are individual amino acids linked together. How long they are and which format they take will dictate what protein they will be, meaning there are masses of different combinations and therefore proteins

in food. It is elements in individual proteins that can generate an immune reaction and as our immune system is unique to us so will our reaction to different foods which is why food intolerances can cover virtually the entire food spectrum and why everyone who is food intolerant has a different mix. A protein called casein is suspected as a main intolerance protein. Although it is found naturally in milk it is also used in many processed foods and products, many times as a hidden ingredient.

When the immune system has accepted certain elements in a food item as an antigen, it will store all these details in its memory bank and manufacture antibodies. Antibodies are the first line of defence for the immune response.

ANTIBODY PROTECTION

There are billions of different combinations of antibodies floating around continuously in the body. Antibodies are manufactured by a particular immune cell called the B cell. Each B cell is programmed to make one specific type of antibody. The antibodies that trigger a food intolerance are IgG antibodies normally designed to fight other invaders such as bugs and bacteria in deep tissue, especially around the gut.

B cells patrol around the body carrying out surveillance work. If a B cell comes across something large it does not recognize or has reacted to before it will generate a response. The first few may go unnoticed because the immune system only keeps a small number of each type of antibody out on patrol but more of the same will soon attract its attention.

The antibody is a key looking for a lock, one type of antibody matches precisely one particular type of molecule, its antigen. Once the key fits then the antibody attaches itself to the antigen and sets itself up like a beacon. Acting like a flag, it marks the antigen for destruction.

The B cell will then produce millions of identical antibodies which pour into the blood stream to start the destruction process of this and any identical antigens it can find.

Some antigens have almost identical "locks." This near match could be one possible explanation as to why a food intolerance often involves multiple foods rather than just one. If the food is eaten again before all the reaction has finished then the antibodies will be constantly generating a low level immune response generating a persistent problem.

Antibodies are designed to kill alien invaders that are living organisms like bacteria, viruses and parasites. The antibody attaches itself to the antigen and will attempt to kill it. The difference with food is that it is not alive so the antigen cannot kill it. Realising it is having no effect on the antigen, more destructive immune cells are called in.

The antibody, with its attached antigen will locate other sets of attached antibodies and create a clump big enough to be noticed by other immune cells. These cells, known as phagocytes, rush to help.

The first thing a phagocyte will do is completely engulf everything. Internally a phagocyte contains a potent toxic mix of chemicals that should be able to completely dissolve the antigen. If this is the case then the phagocyte will be engulfed by an even bigger immune cell that will neutralise the toxicity of the cell and dispose of it without too much trouble to the rest of the body.

Further assistance comes in the form of a complement. This triggers off a whole series of cascades calling on far reaching immune resources which if all else fails, will literally blow up everything attached to or surrounding the antigen.

WHAT ABOUT WEIGHT?

So far any studies into food intolerance have centred for obvious reasons, around unpleasant, often serious chronic health conditions that have a really detrimental effect on people's lives. The primary concern was to reduce negative symptoms but new research is beginning to show that once some sufferers had eliminated the offending foods from their diet, not only did their condition improve but they also found that their body shape and weight also changed for the better.

In relation to weight, one of the negative affects of a food intolerance is a potential reduction in the amount of nutrients absorbed and utilised by the body. The body will recognise that it is in short supply and sends messages to the brain to order some more. This affect could potentially generate sensations of hunger and increase food craving and intake.

In a balanced system, when we fill up with energy supplies, our body will want to utilise them. We will feel full of energy and want to go off and burn that energy up. With an imbalance present often the more we eat the more lethargic we feel.

The body may be full of energy reserves stored as fat but it may not be able to process them as efficiently or be less inclined to release it. If the body feels under threat or senses an increase in demand it will be more protective of its stored supplies or less able to supply. We all know what happens when there is some sort of potential shortage announced. Everyone goes out and panic buys even if it is something they don't normally use that much. Once we have our stockpile we will be reluctant to use it because we don't know how long the shortage could go on for or how much more we will need if the problem is prolonged. If your body is unsure or unconfident about its future, it will switch into siege mentality and just supply enough resources to keep everything on tick over.

There are more direct reasons why the size and shape of the body may change due to food intolerance. These are nothing to do with calories. Apart from storing fat, there are other reasons why cells inflate and water retention is one of them.

Part of the immune response is to create swelling and inflammation. Both of these reactions cause the cells in the body to expand, altering the external shape of the body. The body will also pump fluid into the cells to dilute toxins and retain fluid to maintain blood pressure and metabolism.

A lot of the weight loss or body shape change that comes from addressing a food intolerance is very rapid because it is simply excess fluid that the body has been hanging onto.

If you suffer from bloating this can have little to do with calories as it often takes up to five days to process them. Gas and excess food bulk from slow processing and excess bad bacteria can generate bloating and an unhealthy gut is often a sign of food intolerance problems.

Weight issues may seem trivial compared to the chronic conditions more associated with food intolerance, but weight is now a major health issue in today's society. Anyone who achieves and maintains a healthy balanced weight and shape also has a greater chance of reducing the likelihood physical and mental health problems.

Match energy levels to food cravings

- Tired half an hour after eating
- Crave high calorie foods when busy
- Comfort eat when you are unhappy or angry
- Become ravenous at 11.00 in the morning or 3.30 in the afternoon
- Eat whatever is available no matter how much is in front of you
- Eat healthily all day but over eat in the evening
- Feel constantly hungry even after a big meal
- Need to snack and pick at food

NOT JUST ONE THING

Tackling food intolerance may well improve your size and shape but you still need to look at the complete picture if you want to maintain a balanced weight. For example there is no point following a food intolerance elimination diet in the hope it will solve your weight problems if you are still eating three bars of chocolate, 5 cream cakes, 10 lattes and a large pizza to go every day.

One of the problems with determining if food intolerance is involved is any symptoms such as bloating, fat storage and fluid retention and any influence it might have on your weight are also similar to other conditions and imbalances such as chemical and enzyme intolerance or insulin resistance.

To make it even more complicated, other conditions can undermine the health of the gut or the immune system and make you more susceptible to food intolerance demonstrating once again that things rarely happen in isolation but from a combination of negative factors over time.

Why No Weight Loss?

ENZYME INTOLERANCE

Specific enzymes break up specific foods into absorbable components in the digestive tract so that they can be absorbed into the body. Without these specific enzymes the food remains unprocessed and remains in the gut causing health problems and leaving the body nutritionally deficient. The most well know is Lactose intolerance and although not common in western cultures, 75% of the worlds population is believed to be effected by it. When lactose is not digested, it remains in the intestine exerting pressure that draws in fluids and salts. This increased level generates an imbalance that encourages bacteria to ferment lactose into the gas hydrogen, associated with flatulence and bloating. Additional salts also add to further fluid retention.

GLUTEN

Coeliac Disease is an inflammatory disease caused by an intolerance to gluten, a protein found in certain cereals particularly wheat and is closely associated with gut disorders such as IBS. Not all Gluten causes Coeliac Disease but can still irritate the gut. Non-Coeliac Gluten Intolerance can also cause similar symptoms such as bloating.

REASONS FOR BLOATING

Fact - studies show that nearly 60% of us suffer from bloating.

Too much bad bacteria – bacteria give off gases that blow the stomach up.

Unrecognized food intolerance – generate swelling.

Yeast – yeast colonises an unhealthy gut and gives off hydrogen.

Slow digestive system – food hangs around in the gut for too long and is slow to pass through leading to discomfort.

Dysfunctional digestive system – gut movement is uncoordinated so food is poorly processed.

Irregular eating – the gut likes consistency and a bit of warning otherwise it gets confused making digestion more difficult.

Fact - apparently only 36% eat 3 regular meals a day

Foods high in fat or heavily processed – they slow the normal digestive process down and clog the system up.

Too much alcohol – puts the digestive system on a go slow and encourages the growth of bad bacteria and yeast.

Eating late at night – like everything else in the body your digestive system needs rest and relaxation to keep it functioning effectively so don't give it a major job when it just wants to go to bed.

Eating on the go – we all know if you try to do more than one job at a time you end up doing a lot of not very good work. Stress diverts energy away from the digestive system leaving it with a long list of jobs unfinished and pending.

Eating with your mouth open – keeping a conversation going while you are eating or chewing gum constantly can bring lots of air into the gut.

Fizzy drinks – many slimmers like no-cal drinks but they are full of gas. Sweetners also have a negative effect on the gut and can increase your level of wind.

Hormonal imbalances – most women have experienced bloating just before a period but the more irregular your hormonal cycle the more constant the problem becomes.

Do you?

- Feel sick or queasy after a meal?
- Feel like a brick is living in your stomach?
- Blow up even though you have hardly? eaten anything?
- Feel uncomfortable?
- Belch?

FLUID RETENTION

Bloating and fluid retention can be viewed as the same thing or go hand in hand but there are additional reasons why fluid retention specifically may be a problem.

Fluid is regulated by the lymphatic system but unlike the circulatory system which uses the heart as a pump to move blood around, the lymphatic system relies on muscle movement. Lymphatic drainage helps remove toxins along with excess fluid from body tissue. Unfortunately legs and especially ankles are prone to fluid retention as the fluid runs down well enough but it is a long climb back up when you rely on muscle contraction. Fluid retention is also associated with the appearance of cellulite, a combination of fat, toxins and fluid that tends to build up mainly on the bum and thighs. Exercise is the key to keeping your lymphatic system flowing but as usual there is more to it than that.

The lymphatic system also moves fat and distributes fat soluble vitamins A,D,E and K. The lymphatic system needs as expected, energy to power it and nutrients to keep it healthy.

Fluid also needs the right balance of minerals to enable it to be utilised or removed. Sodium is the key water-retaining mineral and potassium is the main fluid releasing mineral which is why fluid retention is a problem for people with diets high in salt. Unfortunately salt is generally found in high fat, low nutrition foods where as potassium is generally found in fresh fruit and vegetables.

It may sound a bit mad but dehydration is another cause of fluid retention. We are made up of around 70% water. Muscle has around 75% water but fat only

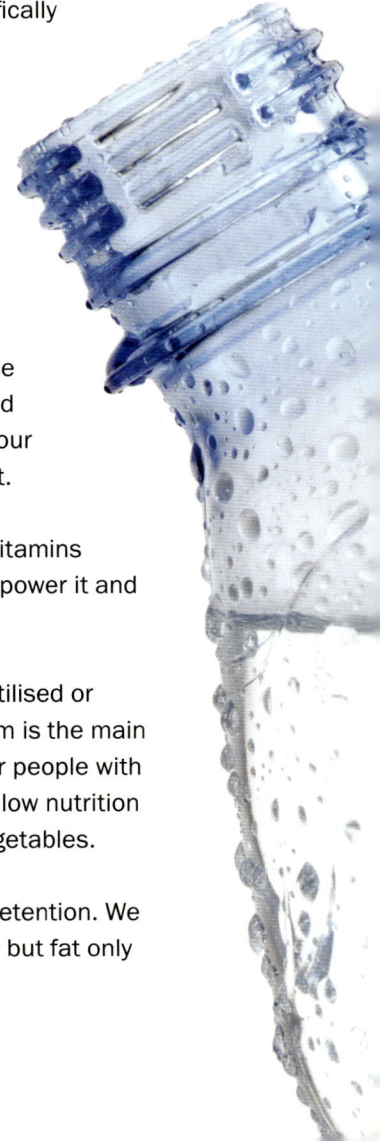

contains around 50% so if you have more fat than muscle it will be harder for you to stay hydrated and avoid fluid retention. Water is used to dilute harmful substances and flush them out, transport energy and nutrients and keep our blood pressure healthy. If you imagine a big hosepipe full of fast flowing water, it will arrive quickly with ample supply and wash anything horrible out of its way. If there was only a trickle then silt would build up, pipe work would get blocked, supply would be very poor and not a lot of gunk would get flushed out.

If the pressure is not there then pools of stagnant fluid could build up leaving you more prone to infection and disease. The kidneys rely on this pressure to remove harmful toxins out of the body in the form of urine. If there is not enough pressure the body cannot release as much urine and more ends up being passed out through skin pores. This creates another unpleasant problem in the form of excess sweating and BO. If fluid retention is a problem then you could be dehydrated and just need more pressure to enable excess fluid to be excreted.

Do you?

- Suffer from constant urinary infections or irritable bladder?
- Have regular night sweats?
- Suffer from body odour?
- Have bad breath?
- Have cellulite even if you are quite slim?
- Have a more pear shaped figure?
- Get fat, swollen ankles?

WHAT COMES FIRST →

The other essential role of the lymphatic system is the facilitation of immune responses. Lymphatic tissue helps manufacture, store, transport and initiate the actions of immune cells. There is growing evidence to suggest the more fat you have the more sensitive you are to inflammation but as yet it is hard to determine which comes first.

We have already looked into reasons why inflammation can lead to bloating and fluid retention, increasing your size and shape but can it also be responsible for fat storage?

TNF-alpha is a key component in the inflammatory response and fat cells are believed to be involved in its formation. Research has shown higher levels of TNF-a in obese people and the theory is that this raises levels of the IgG antibody and increases inflammatory stimulation. Further studies have shown an increased likelihood of inflammatory conditions such as asthma in obese people as antibody levels appear greatly increased.

TNF-a can actually encourage fat metabolism and activate stress hormones which are more likely to encourage your body to burn more fat so how can this increase weight?

Apart from the obvious effect of inflammation encouraging appetite TNF-a is associated with insulin resistance.

Insulin is produced by the pancreas and is responsible for controlling blood sugar levels and fat metabolism. Blood sugar levels are always fluctuating because they are dictated by our eating patterns and actions. When we eat, levels will rise so insulin is produced, removes excess glucose from the blood and stores it as fat. If we haven't eaten for a while or are exercising, levels will fall and fat is then utilised to produce more energy and levels then rise.

TNF-a suppresses insulin in an effort to keep blood sugar levels high but then the pancreas will produce more insulin to compensate. This means more insulin needs to be produced to remove less glucose out of the blood so basically the pancreas is working less effectively. High insulin production leads to low blood sugar levels and you will feel exhausted. This battle may seem odd but not if you remember the body needs to stay in balance. Triggering off a stress response for example is not supposed to be for very long so you need to have a boost to get things sorted and then a system to get everything back to normal. It

FAT OR INFLAMMATION

only becomes a problem if it is sustained, so a constant cause of irritation even at a low level is going to generate an imbalance and maintain it.

Like you, your poor old pancreas becomes exhausted with all the extra work, and over time there is only so much insulin it can produce under such stressful circumstances. Eventually it is so warn out that insulin function becomes impaired, tissue is less able to take up glucose and is instead stored as fat, particularly in the abdominal areas, around essential organs and as fatty plaque in the arteries.

Our ability to utilise insulin varies from person to person but it does seem the more weight you carry the more likely you are to develop insulin resistance and inflammatory conditions. It has been established that a diet high in sugar and fat combined with a sedentary lifestyle increases your risk of insulin resistance dramatically and if not addressed leads to diabetes but only now is a link with inflammation and fat storage starting to emerge.

Signs of insulin resistance

- Sudden drops in energy
- Chocoholic
- Abdominal fat
- Blood pressure problems
- Sugar exhausts rather than stimulates
- Weight gain around the abdomen

Insulin resistance can generate another one of those vicious spirals of negativity which seems to keep cropping up whenever we talk about body balancing. With it you are more likely to put on weight and will find it much harder to lose weight, not just because of internal balances but also because you will have greater cravings for sugary, fatty foods and have sudden drops of energy. Also you will store fat in places that are hard to shift in the abdominal area or develop more cellulite. Unfortunately toxins are also stored in fat so when you do actually start to lose weight, you could feel more exhausted and ill, not the greatest motivation.

Fortunately once you have recognised the problem it is much easier to address as the right diet and exercise plan can make a difference when all else has failed. Also if you know you are going to feel certain things it is much easier to keep those negative responses at bay.

NOTHING IN ISOLATION

Once again we can see how an action, either positive or negative does not result in an isolated, contained incident but triggers off a series of related consequences. For example the development of insulin resistance is usually through a combination of smaller negative actions overtime which eventually changes the way and where fat is stored, increasing not just your risk of diabetes but heart disease and organ damage. It also increases your sensitivity to inflammation, increasing the activation of in particular, IgG antibodies associated with food intolerance. Fluctuations in blood sugar also effects metabolism and the thyroid gland that controls it. This like the pancreas can also be affected by constant stress which can ultimately disrupt the production of metabolic hormones, reducing energy and increasing weight gain with less food consumption. Furthermore, the pancreas is like many things in the body, a multi-tasker. Not only does it manage blood sugar levels it also plays a vital role in the digestive processes, particularly with the digestion of fat and protein. If it is under pressure your ability to process food will also be affected, and as we have already seen, a healthy digestive system is the key to good health.

So a few ongoing negative imbalances can create a whole array of reasons why you might have problems with say, your weight such as low energy, food cravings, increased fat storage, inflammation and poor digestive health. You can also see that weight problems generated in this way are not the root of the problem but a symptom of a much deeper developing health problem.

Fortunately the same cascading formulation applies to a combination of small but positive actions over time. Hopefully you can see by now that food is not just about calories, water is not just about hydration and exercise is not just about burning off fat. They all play a multiple and interrelating part in keeping you fit and healthy. So diet, fluid and exercise have to be part of your life if you want to feel full of energy and maintain a balanced weight but there are also three other aspects you need to include to complete the picture, these are stress, relaxation and stimulation.

THE PHYSICAL FACTORS OF GOOD HEALTH

Diet – why we need a healthy diet – builds body bits, enables your body to function, repairs damage and supplies energy

Water – why we need it – energy, cleans out toxic waste, transports nutrients and energy, gives us a shape, size and flexibility – we are 60 – 70% fluid and without we would just be a foot high solid mass of gunk.

Exercise – why we need it – burns off fat, builds muscle, stamina and keeps lymphatic system going

Relaxation – why we need it – gives body time off to repair itself, get rid of toxins, rebuild and restock resources.

How they interrelate – here are some examples – water transports nutrients, exerc se pumps fat soluble vitamins A, D, E and K, relaxation utilises nutrients, nutrients run body systems, regulate fluid, replaces what exercise uses, creates the right brain chemicals to enable us to relax – the list is endless

THE PSYCHOLOGICAL FACTORS OF GOOD HEALTH

Managing stress – why we need to do it – to keep it in balance, keep it under control and to achieve and succeed, because stress is part of living

How we achieve it – good diet, water, exercise, relaxation, positive stimulation

Experiencing positive stimulation – why we need it – makes it all worthwhile, releases natural feel good responses, keeps us healthy – 20 seconds of hearty laughing is as beneficia as 3 minutes on a rowing machine

How we achieve it – guess what – good diet, water, exercise, relaxation, managing stress

THE PROBLEM WITH STRESS

Today's lifestyles are portrayed as an all work no play frenzy. Apparently we are overloaded with constant negative pressure and stress related health problems. But theoretically life today should be less stressful as compared to even 60 years ago we are richer, safer and more indulgent. Gone are the days when we worked from the age of 9 for 18 hours a day down a mine and still couldn't buy enough food. We have so many time saving gadgets that we no longer have to clean carpets with a tiny brush or only have one dress which takes a whole day to wash. Many of us still have relatives who went through at least one devastating world war and surely there can't be anything more stressful than that. So if all those stressors have been removed making things so much easier now where is all this new stress coming from?

Unfortunately we are still all exposed to the misfortune of experiencing random stressful events. Illness, money problems and unforeseen accidents can suddenly or repeatedly fall out of nowhere landing unpleasantly in our lap but actually most of our ongoing stress comes not from things we are forced into unwillingly but things we actually chose to do such as moving house, having children or improving our career.

Why No Weight Loss?

List out your stress

- Where does it come from?
- Who initiated it?
- Why?
- Is there more than one?
- How long has it been going on for?
- Have you thought of ways to resolve them?
- Are they having an effect on your health?

One explanation why stress today is such a big problem is because we now have more responsibility for our own actions and which life choices we make and the choices appear endless. We could be a millionaire by twenty, have a fantastic career, large family, travel the world, become a professor, and do circus tricks on the side and we feel compelled to do it all at the same time. All this is a very new phenomena, even our parents had to accept a much more limited and predictable life. For women in particular, there was less equality so high-flying jobs were not even a consideration for most and the choice was limited between a small range of careers, marriage, children and looking after our men. Men were also more likely to have a job for life but probably uninspiring with a lower but consistent pay packet. People were more accepting of less but today we can in theory have it all but this increased level of personal responsibility and choice appears to be increasing individual stress and anxiety. Anxiety starts with making the right choice to beating ourselves up when we don't. We are setting ourselves exceptionally high expectations which we can't always live up to and if we do, the effort involved is huge. It is important to have role models and dreams but too many of us are setting goals that are way beyond our abilities and environmental limitations such as family and financial constraints, making everyday a stress inducing disappointment.

So it is not difficult to see why we put stress into the confusing and contradictory category of "can't live with it, can't live without it." We view stress as an illness, a bad thing that needs to be avoided but then deliberately load our life with multiple stress inducing situations not because we intend to do ourselves in but because we think they will improve our life, make it more exciting and stimulating. Unfortunately this can also ultimately result in disappointment, exhaustion and a big stress problem.

So why are we putting ourselves into stress overload?

The answer is compulsion. We need to be stimulated and our body has an in-built stress response specifically designed to cope with stress as it expects to experience it. Basically stress is a natural part of living, whether it is uncontrollably unavoidable or a bi-product of something actively encouraged. Stress is unavoidable so everyone will experience it but it is how you deal with it that will dictate if it will be a problem or not. Your ability to cope with stress enables you to survive in an unstable world, gives you the incentive to stay alive and motivates you to improve your situation. Stress is a negative thing but stimulation makes you feel good, helps you deal with difficult situations and gives you a purpose and thirst for living. Negative stress symptoms like dissatisfaction and anxiety are warning signs designed to tell you that something is wrong, push you into taking action and motivate you to improve your situation. Overcoming a stressful situation can make you a stronger, more confident person, less fearful and more able to cope with future stresses. Stress symptoms may be unpleasant but they are actually a very essential tool in maintaining mental well being. Lets face it, if we didn't have capacity to be unhappy about our situation we would still be living in dark, damp, dirty caves, wearing a bit of fur and grunting its quite nice really.

Positive stimulation or dealing with negative stress responses successfully leads to the release of feel good sensations that encourage you to want and achieve more of the same and if your life is lacking in positive feedback, you will suffer from negative stress symptoms such as frustration, anxiety, low confidence and depression and this can greatly influence the way to look and feel.

Are you in danger of stress?

Do you say things like

- Never enough time in the day
- Running around like a headless chicken
- Life is just one emergency after another
- Things always take longer
- People are always getting in my way
- Life is one chore to another

Then you could be suffering from active stress and need to get some time out

- I always feel dissatisfied
- I am constantly fed up
- I feel stuck in a rut
- Life is no fun
- I feel isolated
- I get no support

Then you could be suffering from passive stress and need to get more positive stimulation in your life

THAT BALANCE THING AGAIN

Not surprisingly, control and balance are the two key aspects of managing stress. The negative effects of stress occur when you do the same action for too long or to an extreme and this equation also explains our love hate relationship with stress. Like overloading one side of a set of scales, too much pressure on one side results in excessive strain and too little on the other makes it weak. In life our stress balance can be upset by too much work and no home life, too much inactivity and little action or too much responsibility and no fun. Experiencing the stress is not necessarily the problem, the imbalance of it is.

When stress responses are balanced they provide the capabilities to keep us alive and happy. Without stimulation we would quite literally not get out of bed in the morning. We are meant to utilise our stress response and thrive off the positive stimulation it can generate. In fact many people suffer from negative symptoms of stress because they are under stimulated and experiencing little pleasure. On the other hand, even positive stimulation of our stress response needs huge amounts of energy and nutritional resources to power them, constant excessive amounts leads to an exhausted body, unable to function properly. The body cannot work to it's full capability if it is tired, making you less able and increasing the likelihood of accidents and mistakes, raising stress levels further. Feeling exhausted and unable to cope as problems escalate leaves you feeling powerless and fearful so it is not surprising you end up bursting into tears and hiding behind the sofa. This is why balance is so important but it is not just about finding a healthy balance but knowing how to maintain and improve it so that you never get extremes of being either bored and under stimulated or exhausted and over stressed.

ARE YOU ACTIVE OR PASSIVE

A healthy balance comes from knowing how to deal with imbalances rather than trying to make life stress free. Are your negative symptoms more in the bored or strained zone?

If you feel constantly under pressure, feel everything is a chore, sleep badly, eat irregularly, need alcohol or cigarettes to help you relax then you could be experiencing Active Stress. Doing too much of everything has physically worn out your stress response and you desperately need to rest so your imbalance stems from excessive stimulation.

If you feel constantly tired, miserable, apathetic, de-motivated, inactive and have problems over eating then you could be experiencing Passive Stress. You are mentally under stimulated so your imbalance stems from lack of positive stimulation Too much stress and stimulation and you burn yourself out physically and too little stimulation generates anxiety, leaving you emotionally stressed out. Like all things with the body, stress needs to be managed to keep a healthy balance. This is relaxation's role. Periods of sleep and relaxation are how your body fixes the damage from stress and replenishes drained resources. The working relationship between your stress response and relaxation is your natural, in-built balancing system. Without relaxation, constant stress will result in a tired and unhealthy body and mind, not equipped to cope with further negative stress or get any pleasure from positive stimulation. Balance enables you to experience the benefits of stimulation but still deal with negative life pressures.

Stress summary

- Stress is a negative thing, too much for too long will generate imbalances that lead to ill health
- The stress response is your body's in-built system designed to cope with negative stress but also to encourage positive stimulation by releasing feel good responses in the brain when something goes well
- Too little positive stimulation can generate stress related symptoms such as depression and anxiety
- Relaxation is needed to rebalance the body after periods of stress or stimulation

Why No Weight Loss?

THE ROLE OF RELAXATION

Every day we set ourselves a to do list and it is the stress responses job to activate the body into action and sort things as quickly and as effectively as possible. Long term health is not a concern of the stress response as it could be dealing with an immediate life threatening situation and if that means using all your resources up in one hit, so be it. Anyway the body knows that during relaxation later it can clean up, repair damage and replace resources. During our daily sleep the body is rebalanced through replenishment and repair, ready for the next busy day ahead. A healthy body should wake up refreshed but by the end of a stimulating day, feel tired because energy supplies have been used and wear and tear has been incurred. Your body switches you off at the end of the day so that it can concentrate on restoration, recovery and regeneration to enable you to go out and live life to the full the next day.

RELAXED? – ME!

- I'm too busy to relax – relaxation is not an indulgence it is a necessity if you want to lead a happy, healthy stimulating life

- I feel tired all day but can't sleep at night – your loss of energy levels are causing you to feel anxious so although you are less active you are still generating stress

- I could sleep for days but still feel tired when I wake up – doing too much during the day could be making it hard for your body to get all its jobs done during the night

- Relaxing makes me feel awful – this is the first sign that your stress is getting too much for your body to cope with

- Instead of relaxing I think of all the jobs I should be doing – then you are not relaxing if you restock your energy levels then jobs will be much easier and quicker to do

- When I feel tired I crave for junk food– you are looking for stimulants when all your body wants is a rest

STRESS IMBALANCE

Stress can have a detrimental effect on any part of the body, including your weight because if unmanaged it can generate biological imbalances. Stress triggers off a chemical response which makes the body run in a different way. The adrenal glands release a range of hormones, including Adrenaline. From a weight point of view initially Adrenaline rushes are very appealing because it activates fat conversion into energy. It is this additional energy that makes you feel fantastic and when we are inactive our body craves for more of the same. Adrenaline can basically save our life by focusing our mind and giving us a level of energy we didn't know we had and it can makes us feel lively and motivated which is great but this energy has to be found from somewhere, at a cost. Adrenaline was only designed to be released in short, sharp doses and this way it can benefit health, especially if it gets you out of a life threatening situation!

The longer it is sustained or the more regularly it occurs, the greater the wear and tear on your body and the faster it will drain energy supplies. High levels of stimulation need high levels of body maintenance and energy production to keep it from harm and too much stimulation for too long without a break is unsustainable. Going back to insulin resistance, stress triggers off an increase in blood sugar or excess sugar can trigger off a stress response, either way a battle will emerge between adrenaline and insulin, one trying to release glucose into the blood and the other trying to get rid of it. It is this constant over production that leads to the problems of insulin resistance such as weight gain and low energy.

STRESSED OUT ON FOOD

So stress can cause blood sugar imbalances and a diet high in sugar and fat can trigger off a stress response. Unfortunately this is only too common in today's society where we have seen the rapid rise in a new "type" of stress generated purely by diet alone. Western diets are particularly high in sugar, fat and refined carbohydrates which we know is not a healthy balance. We also generally drink more alcohol, caffeine and fizzy drinks and we know this combination is not good for the general health of the body, in particular the digestive system. But this kind of diet also continuously raises blood sugar levels which not only increases the risk of insulin resistance, food intolerance and other imbalances it also over stresses the body. Firstly there is a constant triggering off of stress responses when highly stimulating food is eaten, this puts a strain on the adrenal glands and like the pancreas and thyroid, it can only take so much. Secondly the lack of suitable nutrition means your body is less able to cope with internal problems and thirdly the combination of the two means your energy levels

will be greatly reduced and this will make it much harder for anyone to cope with the normal everyday stresses of living. They then believe that life is too stressful when in fact it is perfectly normal, they just don't have the resources to cope with it. Finding it hard to cope, they reduce their levels of positive stimulation, feel fed-up and de-motivated and then start to crave for high fat, sugary stimulating foods to compensate for the lack of pleasure and achievement in their lives, I can feel one of those negative spirals emerging.....!

Can you match your stress to your diet?

FOODS THAT STRESS
· Sugar
· Fatty foods
· Coffee
· Alcohol
· Refined carbs

■ Eating these foods gives me an immediate high then I crash - you are in danger of over loading your system

■ Eating these foods makes me feel exhausted - your system is already overloaded

MORE STRESS

One of the ways Adrenaline comes up with more energy is not to manufacture more but to divert energy away from other areas of the body temporarily. Key areas are the skin, sexual organs, renal system and you've guessed it the digestive system. In normal circumstances the body allocates energy to all areas of the body but under stress the muscles and brain need loads so systems shut down, for example we go as white as a sheet when scared witless, don't think about sex or going to the loo. Not a priority at that present time but once the scary thing is removed the balance is restored. Bursts of stimulation are in fact beneficial to your weight because it burns off fat and makes you less interested in eating. Although most stress today is less scary it is also less active and more constant, depriving and draining the digestive system of valuable energy and resources for long periods of time which is, as we already know not good for our size, shape or general health.

There is constant wear, tear and damage happening internally through the natural process of metabolism

Why we need diet and relaxation to repair cells keep the balance between feeling energized and feeling tired from cellular damage. Here are 3 well known explanations which are actually all part of the same process:

Oxidation – oxygen and glucose are the two key components of energy. The chemical reaction of two molecules meeting generates a micro explosion which gives us our energy but also can cause damage to our cellular structure.

Free radicals – bit like a pinball machine, rogue atoms looking for a mate – they split up other groups and this creates more lost soles that go around bumping into cell walls and causing damage.

Toxins – natural organic bi-product of energy – acid based which burns into cells, causing damage. They form crystals which also clog up the system making it harder for essential nutrients and energy to move around and release energy from cells, so the brain finds it easier to ask for a chocolate bar.

If a stress is prolonged the body then moves from the initial short term stress response to a long term adaptive coping strategy which encourages the body to store more fat. Stress is a high energy user and if the problem is long term the body has to go into preservation mode. Even though it is tired it is less inclined to provide energy boosts and more likely to try and stash it away. Long term stress also generates internal cellular damage which makes fat to energy conversion even less effective encouraging the compulsion to eat more high calorie, fat and sugar foods even greater.

ENERGY CRAVING

From the busy body's point of view foods high in calories, sugar and fat are great, they give immediate energy with little processing. The body was designed a huge number of years ago when finding food, in particular these kinds of foods were a problem so there wasn't really the need to build in some sort limitation signal from the brain, eating was to be encouraged. Yes the brain does have devices to say when we are full but it is fairly primitive. Most of us know it can be over-ridden and it doesn't really bother with dietary balance. Long-term the only real indicators of poor diet are state of health, energy levels and weight. Today's society appears to be not that brilliant at reading these signs by which time the emergence of additional problems such as food intolerance or insulin resistance can make it much harder to determine what our diet requirements should be because we now have to consider personal factors along side a general healthy balanced diet. As an example, say the meal you have just eaten is 25% easy energy from refined carbs, sugars and fats which go straight into the blood stream and be used as an immediate supply. The other 75% will take longer to process but will end up being taken up by cells and released slowly, providing energy long after the meal has gone. In a healthy system, the indication that a sustainable energy supply is available will encourage the body to go out and use it making you feel lively and restless to be active. If processing is poor the body will have trouble utilising the larger amount of slow release and stored supplies of energy making you feel tired and less inspired. Your body will also become more dependent on the smaller amounts of immediate energy found in each meal and the foods that supply them.

Result

- You will be unable to maintain a continuous supply of energy

- Energy levels will fluctuate dramatically throughout the day

- You will only get an energy boost when you eat making you more inclined to snack and increase your food intake

- A habit will form where your body becomes dependent on easy energy food sources

- Slower produced energy sources will be harder to process putting a strain on your digestive and immune systems

- Less fat will be utilised as energy

- Low energy levels will force the body into short term coping strategies – not only will you be more inclined to crave for foods that are high in sugar and fat like chocolate, biscuits and cheese you could also turn to other stimulants such as alcohol, salt, nicotine or caffeine

- The imbalance that created these cravings has now put your body into an unhealthy way of functioning generating further work, wear and tear on the body, weight gain and fatigue

- Overload and stress on the body's systems, especially digestive and immune increases the risk of health and wellbeing problems

- Your emotional state will become more imbalanced leading to mood swings, anxiety and irritability

- Food becomes not just an energy requirement but your main form of comfort

Non-calorie weight gainers

Just because they don't involve any calories doesn't mean to say they can't overload the system and potentially add to weight and shape issues - factors include:

- Smoking
- Low calorie fizzy drinks
- Caffeine
- Sleep badly
- Working long hours
- Too many chemically based toiletries and cleaners
- Live in a city

Irregular eating or living

If the body has no regular eating pattern or your life does not have a structure to follow then it cannot estimate how much energy it will need to deal with your demands or when the next supply will be coming in. This encourages it to hoard supplies and filter out only the bare minimum. When food comes along, your instinct will be to eat as much as possible because your body does not know how much energy it will need in the future or when the next supply will be along. Think holiday buffet — are you programmed to get as much as you can before it all goes?

Your favourite foods

- If you love sugary, fatty, salty foods, can't get enough of them and can't limit your intake if they are easily accessible then this is a sign of an imbalance, increasing your long term risk of developing health problems such as food intolerance or insulin resistance

- If you love vegetables, fish, lean meat and fruit and crave them when you are tired then your balance is good and your body knows it!

EMOTIONAL ENERGY

From an energy point of view it is not difficult to see why we subconsciously crave what we class as the "wrong foods" such as chocolate and chips but consciously most of us just love these foods because they taste fantastic. We should and do enjoy these foods and if they are part of a balanced diet we shouldn't feel guilty about eating them but many of us struggle with the balance thing. We know that eating too much of any one food is not good for health but there are no public health warnings on lettuce because no one really wants to OD on it. So why are such delicious foods so tormenting?

LOVE FOOD

Way back in evolution food was hard to get hold of so it was just a case of pure survival. To encourage us to go out into a big scary world and find food we needed some motivation. If food tasted awful, you wouldn't be very interested in getting and eating it, not a good tactic for keeping the species alive. Sending out pleasure signals when food is eaten is a very good way of getting you to keep yourself alive. We love the anticipation of eating as much as the act itself and as food was scarce, the higher the calorie the greater the pleasure response. This means that most of us do not have a problem eating large amounts of chocolate, chips, biscuits and cakes. So there are actually two very good reasons why we like food so much, one is energy and the other is because it makes us happy. We are supposed to enjoy food otherwise the human race would have died out years ago because we all know we will not eat anything we do not enjoy. Unfortunately a lot of our health problems today are due to the fact that foods high in calories, fat or sugar are so readily available and not because they are necessarily unhealthy. Also if you are unhappy and anxious with your life you will find that you are more likely to crave these foods as they become a rare source of pleasure and satisfaction.

If you are unhappy with your life, the way you look or feel, or are tired all the time, maintaining a low calorie diet could prove impossible because all your body wants you to do is continue eating and because this makes you feel even more miserable, you turn to food not just for energy but because you feel unhappy.

Your happiness scale
Questionnaire

- Do you feel guilty about having time out to enjoy or relax?
- Do you always put other peoples demands and wishes before your own?
- Do you find it hard to say no?
- Do you feel life is one long chore or duty?

- Do you ever deliberately make arrangements to do something enjoyable?
- Do you think happiness is important to your own health?
- Are you happy with the way you look?
- Do you have lots of confidence?

If you answered yes to any of the first 4 and no to the second 4 then you have a low happiness scale.

Emotional feelings of pleasure and satisfaction are vital for physical health.

PLEASURE PRINCIPLE

It seems if you want to appear grown up you first have to fill your life with endless chores and duties that keep you constantly busy and do things because you have to or must do. Having dreams, desires and fun is frowned upon as being indulgent, frivolous and pointless and not something that busy, sensible grown ups have time to do. Doing something just for the fun of it makes you feel guilty and defensive, fabricating excuses to justify your actions when you do something that has no other purpose but to bring pure gratification. Obviously I am not suggesting we all abandon our responsibilities, strip off naked and run down the street shouting I don't care anymore but experiencing pleasure and satisfaction is the most fundamental requirement of good health and lack of it can result in stress, poor health and weight gain.

We were not designed to do purposeless must does, we are designed to do things because they have the potential to improve our life. The human race hasn't stayed around so successfully for this long because it has had to but because we have wanted to, surviving in an extremely difficult environment has been entirely through our own choice. To survive we have to achieve, take risks, experiment, cope with trauma, get on socially and do things that are not very pleasant and to encourage us to do this we need an incentive. This incentive is the ability to experience positive feelings such as happiness and contentment. We need to set goals, have dreams and ambitions, change our situation, socially interact and we do all this hoping that it will make our life that little bit better. We often feel guilty about taking time out to have fun but experiencing pleasure and satisfaction is the greatest health tonic of all. It fills you full of energy, burns fat and keeps you motivated. In fact a recent study discovered that 20 seconds of hearty laughing is as beneficial to your health as 3 minutes on a rowing machine, so not difficult to guess which one I will be doing more of!

If food has become your main source of pleasure then you have been neglecting your natural ability to experience pleasure and satisfaction from living. You need to make time to enjoy life, have fun and achieve more rewarding goals. Are you happy being in love with food, does it make you feel good? If the answer is no then you need to find a healthier passion.

LIFESTYLE OR BIOLOGY?

Hopefully by now you should be able to answer this question as either but more likely both.

FOR EXAMPLE:

Lifestyle factors such as poor diet, smoking and stress undermine the health of the body, undermining energy levels, gut health and over sensitizing emotions and immune systems, increasing the risk of a range of chronic health problems including food intolerance.

An unrecognized condition such as a food intolerance can undermine the health of the body, undermining energy levels, gut health and over sensitizing emotions and immune systems leading to a range of persistent health problems such as weight and shape issues.

Unhealthy body imbalances such as being overweight can undermine the health of the body, undermining energy levels, gut health and over-sensitizing emotions and immune systems leading to unhealthy lifestyle practices such as comfort eating which then lead to gut problems and increased food sensitivity.

Balancing your pleasure responses

Basically there are two ways to trigger off a pleasurable response

1. **Emotional** - from doing things with your life that give you a high

2. **Chemical** - food and stimulants such as alcohol

A happy, healthy balanced life has a high percentage of the first one and then only needs a small amount of the second. Think of those annoying people who are happy to eat only two chocolates out of a whole box!

When things go wrong in life it pollutes other areas of happiness. For example if you lost your job, your unhappiness could prevent you from getting enjoyment from friends, hobbies and family as it is hard to keep emotional responses up.

Chemical responses on the other hand will always give you a high and if you are not getting pleasure from living then your brain will demand you get it from food and stimulants.

EVERYONE AND YOU

Hopefully by now you can see that finding the weight you want is through a combination of actions involving food and fluid, positive stimulation and activity, relaxation and stress management. These actions should be based on information that relates to us all but then refined to suit your own individual requirements. So eating more veg for example, is good for us all but you may hate the taste of onions, cabbage makes you burp or parsnips bring you out in a rash.

This may initially seem a lot to remember but actually finding out what suits you is relatively straight forward, a lot of it is stuff you probably already know or just basic commonsense, it is how you link it together that makes the difference between a successful plan of action and a random, confusing and conflicting collection of information such as eat more wheat its full of goodness, don't eat wheat it makes you bloated and triggers intolerances.

There are also less obvious imbalances to consider. For example we all know that eating too many cream cakes is going to increase weight but you perhaps didn't realize where the compulsion was coming from. If you understand why you have cravings and have alternative plans to follow, things become much easier to manage.

TIME TO THINK ABOUT YOU

The first step is to give yourself time to read the clues your body is already giving you. Basically you need to think about you.

Look specifically at your weight – where is it, how much is there?

Do you also get fluid retention – where – bloating – where?

Are there already foods you avoid – why – what are the negative symptoms – can you be sure it is that food in particular?

Do you have any other negative symptoms:

- Fatigue

- Bladder problems

- Poor skin

- Digestive problems

- Irritability and mood swings

- Poor concentration

- Muscle and skeletal aches

Do you need to lose weight?

- Do you have poor body image?
- Are you using your weight as a scape goat for other more difficult problems?
- Are you a perfectionist and weight has become an obsession when you should be just enjoying life?
- Could you just accept who you are and make the most of what is good in your life?
- You need lots of motivation to change your life, what's yours?
- Is that strong enough?

Energy

- What's slowing you down?
- Is your life on a go-slow or are there not enough hours in the day?

Satiety foods

- What is your appetite like?
- Are you hungry all the time and never feel full?
- Or only when food appears?
- Eat lots but don't really taste it?

Emotional relationship with food

- What are your emotional associations with food?
- What do you crave?

Also practical

- Be honest, what is your diet really like?
- Do you give up in the first few days of a diet?
- Do you think you are in denial?
- Are you double eating or eat out of balance?
- Do you eat a lot of slimming ready meals?

MAKE CHANGE HAPPEN

NOTE: if you are thinking of making any changes to your diet or lifestyle we always advise you consult a doctor or appropriate health professional first and do it under the supervision of a health professional – this is imperative if you suffer from an existing medical condition. Never go on a weight loss diet if you are pregnant.

Children should never follow adult designed weight loss eating programmes.

You have to know where you are starting from and this means you have to be honest with yourself. For example, admit you over eat, get less exercise than you think or do feel tired.

■ Set yourself a goal – what is it you want to achieve? If you just want to be happier then is weight loss going to achieve that?

■ Draw up a plan of action - that is realistic and includes what to do when things go wrong. Don't ignore your limitations work with them, accept that things don't always run to plan, life isn't perfect so don't expect it to be.

■ Break it up into small, manageable steps - things never get done if the job is too big and scary, give yourself small, achievable weekly targets that are easy to implement.

■ Keep assessing your progress - so you can change things that aren't working. Rigid plans can be demoralizing, if something isn't working you need to know as soon as possible.

■ Keep your options open - always have alternatives because you never know what you like until you try it. Always have a plan B in hand to move onto otherwise you will just give up if something goes wrong.

■ Don't get stuck in a rut - be prepared to experiment but only if it is safe to do so. For example, don't think you have to go to the gym to get fit, list up a range of sports to try out so if you don't like one you can move onto something else, remember this has to be enjoyable otherwise it won't be sustainable.

■ **Accept there will be things that won't change** - or change as much as you would like but if you make other aspects better then this will dilute their negative impact. All your problems do not suddenly disappear just because you are losing weight but feeling healthier is going to help you deal with them more effectively.

■ **Don't beat yourself up if you don't reach your targets** - work on the principle that any improvement no matter how small is better than nothing. Just ask yourself what happens if I don't do it.

■ **You can always learn from any experience** - even if it wasn't a very nice one. People who have experienced success will tell you they learnt the most from what didn't work. If you know what doesn't work then in principle if you do the opposite, it will.

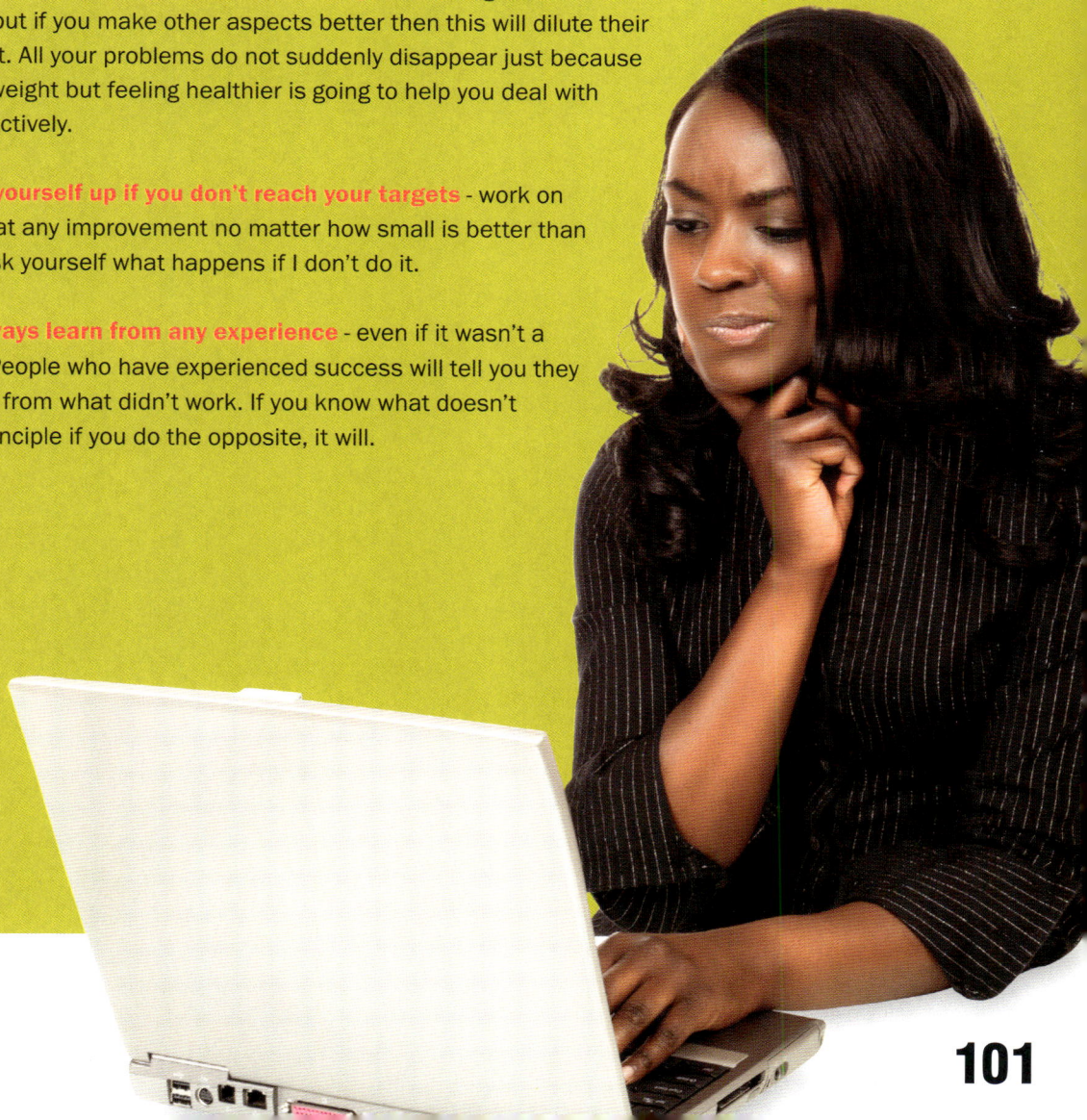

DIET FOR GOOD HEALTH

All bodies have specific nutritional requirements and yours is no different. Firstly you need to use this as a base diet and then when you have found your individual requirements you can omit them from this basic format and find alternatives to fill the gap.

BASIC FOOD GROUPS

VEGETABLES – veg are great, they are packed full of a whole range of nutrients and are generally low in fat and calories. If you want to lose weight then these should account for the majority of your diet. The only ones you really need to watch are pulses such as lentils and root vegetables, particularly potatoes as they have a higher carbohydrate and calorie ratio but even so you would still need a bucket full of carrots and parsnips to reach your allotted daily calorie intake.

MEAT – lean meat is an excellent source of protein, vitamins and minerals and if you like eating meat I am not going to stop you. If it is lean and pure it can have less fat than some fish. The meats that really should be avoided are processed meats such as burgers, sausages and pate usually because they use high fat cuts and if that's not enough, add more fat to bump the weight up.

FISH AND SEAFOOD – fish is full of essential fatty acids, the fat you really do need and has loads of other body building nutrients also packed in. Fish can be divided into two groups, white and oily. Oily has a high density of Omega 3 oils but higher in calories and white fish is low in fat. All are an excellent source of protein. As with meat it is not the fish but the things it gets processed with that makes it less healthy.

EGGS – eggs are a great source of protein and also contain a range of body building nutrients. If you think about it an egg is really a big cell designed to grow into a fully formed bird so it has to contain all the nutrients needed in that process.

DAIRY – as milk is designed to provide young with all the nutrients it needs then it is full of body building nutrients but it also has a high fat content. Fortunately skimmed milk has more calcium than full fat but unfortunately less Vitamin D so once again it is about balance. Milk can be an irritant for some people but if you do not test intolerant to it or have any other adverse effects it can be a beneficial part of healthy eating.

FRUIT – fruit is often grouped with vegetables but veg are about 3 times more nutritious than fruit. The fruit is the bit the plant wants us to eat so it fills it full of sugar and water to make it tasty and saves most of the nutrients for the seed, nut, plant or root stock. On saying that fruit still has plenty of nutritional value but if you have sugar cravings or bloating, too much fruit could be an issue. High intakes of citrus fruit in particular such as in fruit juices can also upset the gut.

NUTS AND SEEDS – nuts and seeds are often avoided by dieters because they are high in calories but they have some of the highest nutritional densities of any food. They are the plant version of an egg, the germination of a new plant so they are packed full of nutrients including fibre and protein. Because of the fat content, to lose weight you do need to limit your intake but as they are so satisfying, you fill up much sooner than you would with something like chocolate or biscuits.

CEREALS – many of us have forgotten there is more to cereals than just wheat. Oats and rice in particular are a very good alternative source of carbohydrate but unfortunately cereals are also the basic food source that is used heavily in processed food. Mass produced confectionary, ready meals and the like are often bulked up with cereal and there is no doubt that western diets are far too high in cereals so this group of foods needs to be regulated to maintain a balance.

WATER – water is essential for good health. What you need to remember is that a large proportion of our body is water, not coffee or gin and tonic but water. You put water in with something else and it has to process that first. It can also change the way water is utilised, for example coffee and alcohol are diuretic so you might be putting fluid in but it will come out more quickly, leaving behind chemical and toxin residues. If you crave sugar, fizzy drinks with sweeteners will do nothing to reduce your sweet tooth as they can be a thousand times sweeter than sugar.

PROCESSED AND REFINED FOODS

The list of foods in the previous section are all what I call pure basic foods because they are so natural they don't even need a label. These are the foods our body was designed to eat so there is less stress on your system. The majority of processed foods are high in calories but have little nutrition apart from high levels of carbohydrate. Usually this carbohydrate is also heavily refined, making it even less nutritious and more stressful on the body. Refined wheat for example, found in white bread can be so refined it has the same effect on blood glucose levels as white sugar.

BALANCE

The standard dietary advice for a balanced diet is 50% carbohydrates, 35% fat and 15% protein. This may seem simplistic but actually it is hard to follow as all foods have a range of fats, proteins and carbohydrates in them and even I couldn't reel off every food ratio, even if I wanted to be that bothered. For example almonds, oats and peppers contain carbohydrate, fat and protein in varying ratios so its not just a case of one food fits into one category. This percentage ratio also only really applies to maintaining weight and not losing it.

PLATE and HANDFUL

For weight loss it is much easier to work directly with the foods themselves.

If we put food into categories

The top food group would be – coloured vegetables, that's all veg apart from potatoes and pulses. These are your "free range" category, the major part of your diet. Call this section **A**.

For example imagine your food on a plate. If half of your plate is vegetables, excluding root potatoes and pulses and another quarter, section **B** is either potatoes, pulses, or cereals such as pasta then the remaining quarter, section **C** is for lean meat, white fish or for something out of the handful category.

For foods that are high in protein but may also be high in fat such as oily fish, nuts or grated cheese, for a meal these could be a section **C** alternative. For breakfast foods, packed lunches or ones more likely to be eaten as a snack such as fruit, nuts and seeds you can also use the handful rule. 1 egg or one apple will fit in the palm of you hand so that makes one serving but you can also say a handful of nuts or berries.

THE USUAL ODD POINTS

Obviously milk or natural plain yoghurt is a bit messy in a handful so 125ml is a good guide which is about a quarter of a pint, an average pot or half glass.

For high fat foods such as olive oil, sunflower oil, butter or salad dressing use a level teaspoon per serving. This obviously means you can't deep fry anything!

This will give some idea of a balanced diet without having to work out which and how much are carbs, proteins or fat in each food. If you are preparing a meal which combines food such as pasta or shepherds pie you will find it easier to divide the food before you prepare it.

Food Ratio

Typical Western Diet

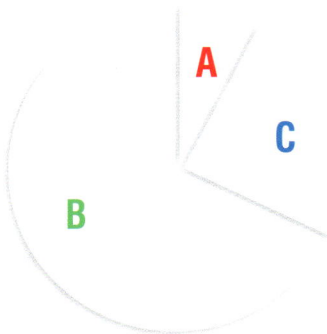

A
C
B

Weight Loss Diet

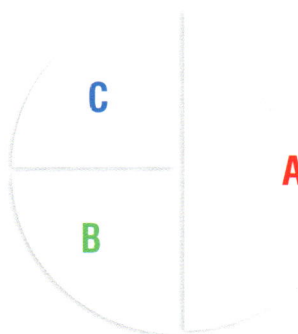

C
A
B

Maintenance Diet

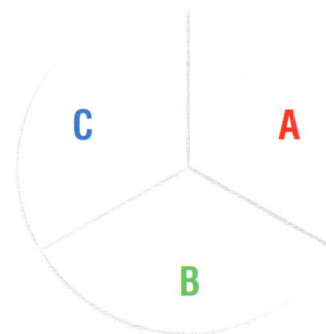

C
A
B

A - Vegetables (except potatoes and pulses)
B - Potatoes, pulses and cereal foods (such as bread and pasta)
C - White fish or handful foods - oily fish, meat, nuts, seeds, dairy, eggs, fruit

MEALS

The body hates irregular meals, giving it 3 meals a day will make it feel more in control and secure about where and when nutritional supplies will arrive. You can also have 3 snacks a day.

Make sure each section has a different item in it and handful items vary for different meals and snacks.

If we follow the plate and handful rule.

BREAKFAST – 3 HANDFULS – Handful of nuts and seeds, yogurt and a pear

Boiled egg, slice of wholemeal toast and a handful of dried fruit

LUNCH – PLATE

Tuna, salad and baked potato (handful, half a plate, handful)

Vegetable soup, granary roll, banana (half a plate, handful, handful)

DINNER – PLATE

Lean steak, vegetables and baked potato. (handful, half a plate, handful)

Roast chicken, dry roast vegetables and steamed green veg (handful, handful, half a plate)

Prawn and pasta with vegetables (handful, handful, half a plate)

SNACK – HANDFUL

Piece or handful of fruit

Handful of nuts and seeds

DON'T EAT ANYTHING THAT YOU KNOW YOU ALREADY REACT TO, DON'T LIKE EATING OR DON'T EAT FOR MORAL OR RELIGIOUS REASONS.

Why No Weight Loss?

VARIETY

From a biological point of view the body needs a wide range of foods to achieve full nutritional status. Eating a varied diet also reduces the risk of the negative effects of food intolerance and eating seasonally provides a more natural diet, one our body is more accustomed to. Variety also makes our diet more satisfying so we are less likely to over eat. We often think we eat a varied diet but actually it can be very repetitive, containing the same kinds of foods but just processed in a different way. This makes our taste buds less responsive and we end up eating without really tasting, making it hard for our brain to know when to stop.

THE 80/20 RULE

Food should be a pleasure and there is no getting away from the fact that foods we class as indulgent such as chocolate are the ones most missed in any weight loss diet. Don't take up the challenge, but I am sure if most of you were force fed nothing but chocolate you would soon grow to hate it. Part of the pleasure of an indulgent food is that it is an occasional treat but feeling guilty about eating it is just going to take away that pleasure. My pet food is chips and when I eat out with friends they accuse me of eating nothing but chips but that's because I only eat them when I go out for a meal, which is about once or twice a month. You can also improve the health aspects of so called "naughty foods." Make homemade oven baked chips, dry roast vegetables, make your own beefburgers with pure lean beef or eat dark chocolate.

In a weight loss plan these indulgences should be reduced depending on how quickly you want to lose weight. When it comes to weight maintenance the danger is of upsetting the balance to the extent that you start to put it all back on again. Being happy with your food is all part and parcel of eating healthy so a good way to maintain the balance is to follow the 80/20 rule. If 80% of your diet is veg, lean meat and fish then you could enjoy 20% selected from the more indulgent categories such as cheese, chocolate and thankfully chips.

Do you eat the same foods?

- Do you notice what you eat?
- Can you remember how much you eat?
- Do you have a regular pattern of eating with the same foods?
- Are there any foods you think make you feel worse?

WHAT ABOUT WATER

This ratio is very good for working out if you are drinking enough water. Its all very well saying you drink a litre a day but if you also have 10 cups of coffee and a bottle of wine that's not too good. If you follow the 80/20 rule and make 80% of your fluid intake water then you can enjoy a glass of wine or a cup of coffee and not feel guilty about it.

FOOD FOR YOU

The diet plan we have just discussed is what fits the average person but we also need to add to that what suits you. Some of you have already applied these rules and still feel frustrated about your weight. You may find the 80/20 rule or the plate ratio doesn't benefit you but these are only guidelines and with a little adaptation you can find the right ratio for you. Whatever your heath problem, be it weight gain, fatigue or IBS eating a general healthy diet is going to generally help everyone with that problem but there will be some of you that need that extra bit of tweaking. If you have hidden food intolerances then foods classed as "healthy" to the majority could be contributing to your problem which is why you are so fed-up and frustrated with it because it just won't go away!

You might have just read through the general diet plan and thought, been there done that, didn't work which means you need to see if something is irritating your system.

FIND THAT MISSING LINK

There is something about your uniqueness that means general rules only apply to an extent, To many this extent is not worth worrying about but to some it can make a big difference to how they look and feel about themselves.

If we look at other reasons why we might experience weight or shape problems, many of the foods listed are either the usual unhealthy suspects such as processed and refined carbohydrates or are ones that should happily sit in the good for you category but for you, this may not be the case.

Foods that encourage

Bloating
- Pulses
- Cereals
- Raw food
- Refined carbohydrates
- Fruit
- Specific food intolerance food

Insulin resistance
- Foods with a high GL
- Refined carbohydrates
- Cereals
- Sugar
- Potatoes
- Fruit

There is so much written about GL foods and full lists can be downloaded from the Internet so I am not going to repeat them here.

Fluid retention
- Foods high in salt
- Sugar
- Refined carbohydrates
- Specific food intolerance food

Bacterial imbalance
- Yeast
- Sugar
- Refined carbohydrates
- Citrus fruit

Food intolerance
- Foods vary from person to person

Any food can trigger an intolerance

With most of the above conditions we can start to see a pattern of foods responsible for more than one condition and this is why there is no need to follow a range of different diet plans. A good healthy diet will benefit a range of health problems including weight gain because usually none of them are there in isolation. Usually it is a series of negative imbalances generating a range of symptoms, weight gain being one of them. Food intolerance is different. Throughout this book we have seen the impact of a poor diet on health and how this can ultimately generate food intolerances by over sensitizing the immune system and destabilising gut health. This can then trigger new food intolerances or activate or maintain existing ones but the problem foods are not a specific group of foods, necessarily unhealthy or a food that relates to everyone, each person that is intolerant will have foods individual to them. Unlike other dietary health problems, this can make it very difficult to detect or manage because general rules do not always give you a comprehensive picture.

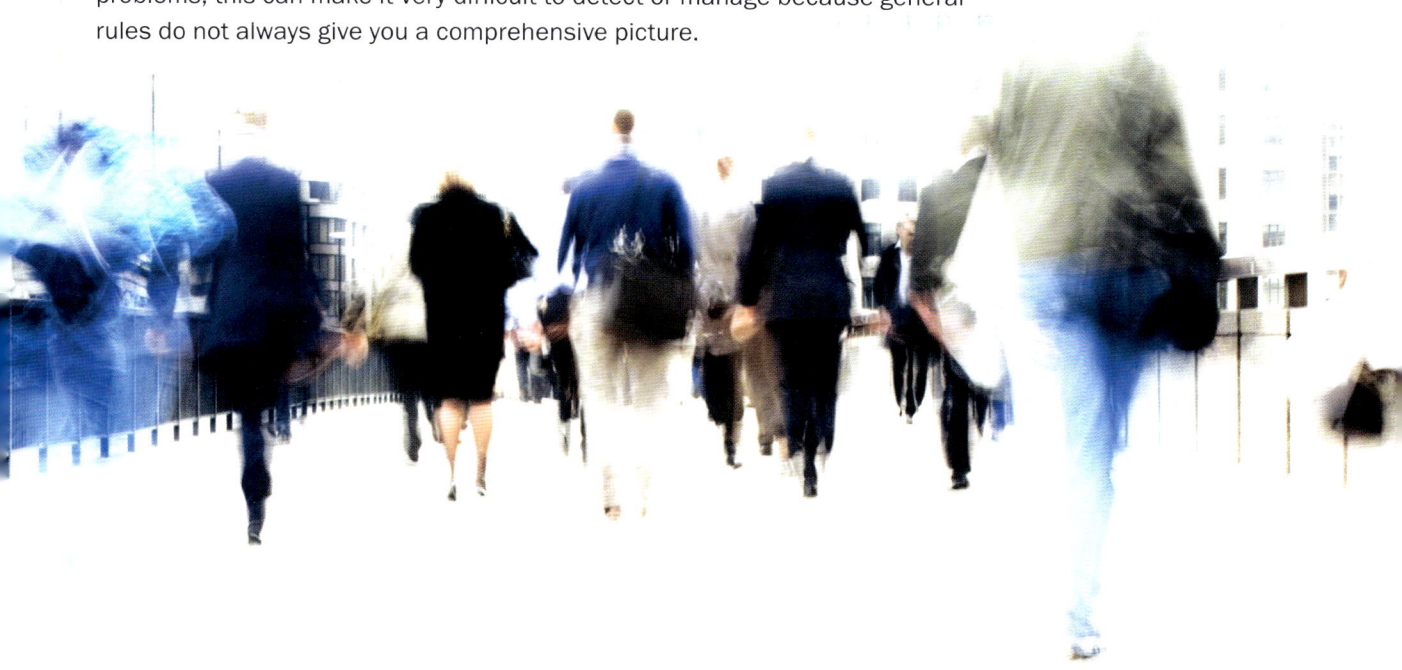

FIND THE FOOD

If following a healthy diet is not producing the results you think it should then food intolerance may be a problem for you. There are two choices in detecting a food intolerance, test **(see page 114)** or elimination diet.

If you want to try an elimination diet then you can only remove one food group one at a time such as dairy, cereals and fruit. You need to do this because if you remove a whole range of suspect foods you will end up with nothing to eat. Take each food or food group, such as eggs or seafood, out of your diet one at a time for a maximum of 21 days. It should be pretty evident by this time if your adverse reactions are still there, that you are still eating the offending food. In this case, nothing in this group appears to be a problem so reintroduce them and move onto another group. If you do improve then something in that group could be a problem food, in which case you need to reintroduce individual food items from that group, one daily for a week and eventually you may be left with an indication of what food it is. Unfortunately with food intolerance there is usually more than one food over a range of groups. Elimination diets are laborious, can take time and are always best done under professional supervision as you may well generate other health problems from destabilizing your diet. You may therefore consider taking a test. Again you need to take care with tests as there are many on the market but not many carry any scientific credentials to back them up.

FOOD INTOLERANCE TESTING

The most reliable food intolerance test to date is a blood test that measures IgG levels against a list of foods. The most well-established and the only test recommended by Allergy UK is YORKTEST's food intolerance test. It has been around for over 25 years and as it has close connections with the scientific community, it has gone through a continuous process of development and research over the years. Unfortunately this testing service did not cater for people who want to see if it could help them with lifestyle related health issues such as lack of energy, weight and body shape issues as it is designed around people with chronic health conditions.

A new service is now available that has been designed specifically for weight loss that combines food intolerance testing with a weight-loss plan.

BODY ID PLAN - SPECIAL SECTION by Dr Gill Hart

The Body ID plan is based around a self administered home finger pick blood test which laboratory-analyses your specific immune response to the food you are eating. Based on the most commonly eaten foods, the test is a well-established IgG antibody test that identifies raised levels in the presence of certain foods, a marker associated with food intolerance.

Your personalised results are combined with a healthy eating plan and lifestyle and motivational advice creating a bespoke plan designed for steady weight loss. The aim is not just to provide a healthy route to weight loss but make it easier to sustain healthy eating by formulating a diet plan that considers what suits you.

Why No Weight Loss?

Basically the Body ID Plan:

- is based on general healthy eating guidelines and your individual biology

- is a personalised approach to weight and shape, taking into account your individual immune response to food

- is combined with lifestyle and motivational advice to provide a comprehensive support pack

- is a quick and easy home test kit combined with laboratory analysis

- provides a long term sustainable eating plan

- offers the potential of additional health benefits from other food intolerant related problems such as low energy

In addition, if the laboratory analysis does not identify any food intolerances you receive a partial refund. For more information on the Body ID Plan visit www.bodyidplan.com

REMOVING FOODS FROM YOUR BASIC FOOD PLAN

Once you have your list of food intolerances, most people have around 3 - 7 so it shouldn't be too scary, compare these with the foods on your basic diet plan. You will need to eliminate these out of your diet but you also need alternatives to replace them. So for example, if one of the foods is wheat, this is found in section B (see page 104), so use alternatives in section B such as potatoes or pulses to maintain the balance. If it is eggs, these are in section C so replace with other items from section C and so on.

You do need to be strict for the first 3-6 weeks otherwise you will not see the benefits but unlike allergies there is a possibility you can reintroduce these foods in moderation in the future. This depends on the health of your gut, overall health and your individual biology. You can start reintroduction 3-6 months after elimination. If your problems return then a least you know what the problem is and can just omit it again.

TOP TIPS TO MAKE IT HAPPEN

1. Review – look at why things have not worked out in the past – can you learn from those experiences? Was it too boring, were you unprepared or were there too many family constraints. If these problems are still there you need to find solutions now otherwise it is unlikely to work again.

2. Preparation – what do you need to do to make sure this new health regime works? Consider what to buy, where from, what are the temptation, dealing with friends and eating out, the right time to start, do you know what you can eat and when. Don't set yourself up to fail, put into place all the things that will make you succeed.

3. Consider health not weight – do you want to feel full of energy or skinny and exhausted? Remember you need to consider all aspects of your lifestyle if you want to achieve maximum results. Are you getting time out to relax, can you take control of your stress, are you getting enough activity, is it interesting enough and most importantly what are you doing to make life happier?

4. Be realistic – actions tend to fail because people are not realistic about what they want. Yes we all want a perfect result in the fastest possible time but in reality this is not how it works. You do need to look at your physical and environmental circumstances and work with your limitations not fight against them. For example, no point setting a target of 2 hours in the gym every day if you work full time and have small children. But you could buy a step meter and walk part of the way to work, take the stairs and do more active things with the kids. If you acknowledge and work within your circumstances you could change them for the better rather than wishing you had something else that was not achievable at the time.

5. Find a plan that suits you – everyone is individual so you need to find the balance that suits you. Remember we are all basically the same but it is our individual differences that can make the normal not work for us. Find the biological and lifestyle imbalances relevant to you and build them in.

6. Sustainability – if you know what your food intolerances, imbalances, diet and lifestyle preferences are you will have a much better chance of sustaining a healthier way of living. It's all about motivation, looking and feeling good comes from the inside. If you get the results then maintaining a healthy eating plan and lifestyle will not be a diet regime or endurance test but a way of living that you have chosen because you prefer it, enjoy it above all the other options available.

Look at it this way, finding a diet and lifestyle that gives you the body you want has got to be worth hanging onto and discovering what works for you personally can make the real difference.

GOOD HEALTH RULES OK

We need:

- diets to be balanced and varied

- adequate intakes of water

- to be active

- positive stimulation

- to manage stress

- relaxation

- to consider what works best for you individually

Remember general rules don't always apply.

NOW IT'S YOUR CHOICE

Ultimately what changes you make to your diet and lifestyle is all down to you, the choice is yours. You can be as strict or as lax as you wish but if you want the best results it pays to stick to a structure, otherwise you will find it hard to know what does and doesn't work for you and this enables you to assess, change and move on. Control will once again be in your hands.

If you are making changes then there will be challenges to overcome. Much better to know how to deal with them beforehand so that if they do appear you know how to limit the negative effects then ignore their existence, meet them full on and despondently give up.

Why No Weight Loss?

REMEMBER it is more likely to be not one thing but a collection of negative elements happening together that fall into two categories:

1. Negative lifestyle factors – you know the sort of thing, an imbalanced diet low in nutrition, stress, alcohol, endless low calorie dieting, lack of activity which is where general rules apply. The diet guidelines in this book are based around a typical healthy diet but you also have to consider......

2. Your personal biology – your uniqueness that can make you more vulnerable to gut problems such as sluggish gut metabolism, poor blood sugar management or food intolerance.

If you feel you have done to death diets then perhaps you have a hidden imbalance and finding your food intolerances could be the missing link in your overall plan for a healthy way of living.

Liz Tucker works as a Health and Wellbeing Consultant, helping others help themselves to a happier, healthier life. Liz is co-founder of the Be Happy Be Healthy Initiative www.behappybehealthy. co.uk and a Health and Wellbeing Consultant for Champneys health resort, running a series of lifestyle health, stress and weight management programmes and has a private clinic at the Hurlingham Clinic. Better known in the media as "The Health Detective", Liz works extensively with the media, writing and contributing to a whole range of mainstream magazines and newspapers including a weekly column in the Sunday Telgraph. She is also a regular on radio and television, most notably as GMTV's Stress Expert and a BBC Breakfast nutritional advisor. Liz's main books in print so far are the Good Health Guide, Understanding Food Intolerances and "When You Want to Say Yes but Your Body Says No," published by Harper Collins. She also conducts "health audits" in the workplace to raise personal health awareness and improve working practices and is regularly employed to give talks, seminars and promote good health.

liz@behappybehealthy.co.uk liztuckerhealth@hotmail.co.uk

"From a child, I always had an allergy to milk but by the time I reached my thirties the toll of firstly student indulgent living and then a workaholic lifestyle led to such a deterioration in my health that I could hardly get out of bed in the morning. After 5 grim years of being told that no one could help me it finally dawned on me that my diet and lifestyle must be playing a part so I totally changed my diet, took more care of my body and dealt with my stress. This made a huge difference but the missing link was finding out what I was intolerant to. I was a guinea pig in the early development of IgG testing working with the scientific founders of what is now YORKTEST. The dramatic change in my health motivated me to go back to university to study human health, biology, psychology and nutrition which is now my passion. Food intolerance is still one of my main professional interests and although my initial interest was to help resolve some fairly nasty health problems, I also found to my delight that I lost loads of weight. Having always been a fat calorie junkie it was a joy to not just reach my target weight but be able to maintain it. Not because I have huge amounts of will power but because I found a way of eating that worked for me."

gill.hart@yorktest.com

Dr Gill Hart has a PhD in Biochemistry and worked as a Senior Biochemist, specialising in endocrinology, at the Hammersmith Hospital, London. She then went on to work for many years in diagnostic test device and automated immunoassays product development, and is now Scientific Director of YORKTEST. Gill is particularly interested in validation and regulation in the self diagnostic testing industry, giving evidence at a recent parliamentary science and technology select committee.

The regulation of food intake in the body is a very complex process, which involves biochemical signals from many sources including the brain, gastrointestinal tract, fat stores and the pancreas. Even the fat cells themselves are very highly specialised to play important roles in energy storage, fatty acid metabolism, and glucose regulation. In each individual there is a very fine balance in energy metabolism stemming from a combination of the intake of readily available food, and overall energy expenditure. However, the relationship between these factors is not always clear cut in such a complex system. Not everyone exposed to a high intake of food, and low energy output will become overweight, and vice versa. What is clear is that increasing adipocyte (fat cell) mass results in an increasing "strain" on important body systems, including the immune system, and alterations in metabolic function. This acts as a vicious circle, and it takes an overall approach to 'undo' any damage caused. This overall approach needs to include identification of any food intolerances.

"For many years we at YORKTEST have seen that people coming to us to help find relief from their chronic conditions have also found that they normalise their weight and shape as a side benefit of changing their diet in response to our food intolerance test. We understand that there are other factors that contribute to weight loss apart from food intolerance, however it is clear that food intolerance as well as food input and energy output all contribute to the fine balance within the body – that makes us what we are."

This book provides a precise and detailed route map for anyone trying to find the eating plan that works for them personally.

Body ID Plan

0800 458 63 93
info@bodyidplan.com
www.bodyidplan.com

Why No Weight Loss?